BUILT
FOR THE AGES

A HISTORY OF THE GROVE PARK INN

BRUCE E. JOHNSON

THE GROVE PARK INN RESORT AND SPA

DEDICATION

This revised edition is dedicated to the resort's true heroes and heroines—the members of our Grove Park family. Whether here for three months or thirty years, each has added a brush stroke to the Grove Park Inn's canvas. Our family is what creates and energizes the magical feeling here.

REVISED EDITION

Copyright © 2004 by The Grove Park Inn Resort and Spa

All rights reserved. No part of this book may be published in any form without written permission from the publisher.

Reprinted in 2006

Published by

The Grove Park Inn Resort and Spa
290 Macon Avenue
Asheville, North Carolina 28804-3799

800-438-0050

www.groveparkinn.com

Jay Boyd, *Director of Marketing*
Julie Powell, *Project Manager and Executive Marketing Assistant*

Produced by Archetype Press

Diane Maddex, *Project Director*
Gretchen Smith Mui, *Editor*
Robert L. Wiser, *Designer*

ISBN 0-9760016-0-8

Printed in Singapore

DISPLAY PHOTOGRAPHS

Back jacket and case binding: This hammered-copper clock once graced the Great Hall.

Page 1: Stones for the hotel's granite walls, some weighing as much as ten thousand pounds, were culled from several nearby mountains and hauled to the site by mule teams in 1912–13.

Page 5: Hotel memorabilia includes postcards, brochures, playing cards, a room key, and a watchman's clock. Also shown are binoculars and an early camera.

ILLUSTRATION CREDITS

All illustrations are from the Grove Park Inn collections except the following:

Page 11 (top), page 12 (left), page 15 (right top), page 36, page 47 (bottom), page 52 (bottom), page 65 (top): Southern Highland Research Center. Page 90: Dan Maxhimer, *Asheville Citizen-Times.* Page 92: Ewart Ball, *Asheville Citizen-Times.* Page 96: J. Weiland.

ACKNOWLEDGMENTS

Since the Grove Park Inn opened more than ninety years ago, several million guests, celebrities, and staff have passed through its front doors, all marveling at the massive boulders in its towering walls and the twin fireplaces in the Great Hall, the craftsmanship evident in the Arts and Crafts antiques and architectural detailing, and the seamless transition between the original main inn (1913) and each of the three additions: the Sammons Wing (1984), the Vanderbilt Wing (1988), and the Spa (2001). Before guests' stays have ended, however, they have also marveled at the graciousness and true southern hospitality that have always been the trademark of the staff of the Grove Park Inn.

I owe a debt of gratitude to hundreds of people, only a few of whom I am able to personally thank. Without their efforts, much of what we know today about the Grove Park Inn would have disappeared long ago. At the top of my list is the entire staff, past and present. Everyone was willing to stop at any time to answer my questions, dig deep into their memories, and share with me their experiences, for they, too, have been touched by this grand old hotel.

This project began in 1987, when I first set foot in the Grove Park Inn and began interviewing people, collecting documents, and gathering information for the original 1991 edition of *Built for the Ages.* I returned a decade later to research this second, updated version. Those who played an important role in this project include the staffs of the *Asheville Citizen-Times,* Biltmore Industries, Pack Memorial Library, and Southern Highland Research Center, as well as the following individuals: Freda Baker, Cynthia Bland, Gertrude Grove Bland, Harry Blomberg, Cheryl Boyd, Jay Boyd, Robert Bunn, Ted Carter, Adella Dilley, Frank and JoAnn Edwinn, David Erskine, Jane Gianvito, Melanie Gidley, Robert Griffin, Robert Hitpas, Troy Hunnicutt, Fred Kahn, Bill Kelley, Ed Leach, J. Craig Madison, Rich Mathews, Richard Maxwell, Gwyn Bellamy McNutt, Patricia Miller, Mary Ashley Morris, Bill and Mildred Neilson, S. M. Patton, Norman and Peggy Payne, Lilian Pierce, Julie Powell, Wilda Robinson, Jane Rowe, Maggie Schlubach, Fred L. Seely Jr., Lorraine Wilson, and many citizens of Paris, Tennessee; St. Louis, Missouri; and, of course, Asheville. I only regret that I did not have the time or the space to interview the hundreds more who could have contributed to this book. I sincerely hope that their information, letters, and memories can be preserved within the Grove Park Inn archives for the next volume.

Finally, I would like to thank Elaine D. Sammons, chairman of the board of Sammons Enterprises, who approved, encouraged, and supported this project and who, more important, has recognized and embraced the role of the American Arts and Crafts movement in the inn's original design. Her efforts to restore and preserve the architectural heritage of the Grove Park Inn, from the historic Great Hall to the most recent additions and renovations, have created not just a highly successful hotel, resort, and spa. They have also confirmed the legacy of the Arts and Crafts movement and the vision of those who built before her: Edwin W. Grove, Fred L. Seely, and Charles A. Sammons.

BRUCE E. JOHNSON

CONTENTS

FOREWORD

At dawn, when the sun breaks the horizon, the first rays of sunshine climb past the top of Sunset Mountain and fall on the red clay tiles of the roof of the historic Grove Park Inn—an event that has marked the beginning of each day at the resort since 1913. But each sunrise is merely a benchmark, a way of keeping track of time; for here at Grove Park, the process is continuous. We never close. When you visit the Great Hall, pause to check the giant oak doors at the entrance. There is no lock. We operate twenty-four hours a day, seven days a week, three hundred and sixty-five days a year.

Within the granite walls of this Grand Lady, I have spent more than half of my own life. During this time the property has gone from a sleepy, seasonal inn—open eight months a year with fewer than forty full-time employees—to one of the top resorts in the United States, with a working family of almost one thousand persons. Today we operate a small city; in fact, our operating budget is larger than that of most towns in North Carolina.

Visitors will see the magnificent features and location that make our resort unique. But something else keeps us here. This Grand Lady has a mysterious hold over us. During the late 1980s, a distinguished ambassador from Japan toured our resort. The granite from which the inn was built, he relayed, has a high concentration of quartz crystals. He suggested that they act like batteries, storing up the life energy of guests and staff and radiating back a special energy. I have often said that it is easy to believe in magic when magicians constantly surround you.

That may be another reason for the special feeling so many of our guests have about the Grove Park Inn: the people who work here. The Grove Park family—and we are truly a family—is an amazing group of hardworking and talented individuals who try to make magic every day. We operate in a culture supported by a vision, with a mission and clear values. During our monthly executive meetings, I can look around the room and count more than 125 years of G.P.I. service at the table. Tenures of three decades and more are milestones seldom reached in an industry with one of the highest employee turnover rates. Robert W. Korba, the president of Sammons Enterprises, Inc., our parent company, says it best: "At the end of the day, it's all about the people!"

You will read about her in this book, but I cannot say enough about the influence of Elaine D. Sammons, chairman of the board of Sammons Enterprises. Simply put, without her and her late husband, Charles A. Sammons, there might not be a Grove Park today. She continues to be the grand matriarch of our family, and we exist here today, and in this grand fashion, because of her.

With several hundred thousand visitors and a thousand members of our resort family, you can imagine that we have our fair share of stories to tell. I hope that you take the opportunity to add your own brush stroke to the canvas of the Grove Park's present, which tomorrow will become a part of our history. The adventure begins anew each day, when the sun's first rays fall down Sunset Mountain and onto the red clay tiles of the historic inn.

J. CRAIG MADISON, *President and Chief Executive Officer*

Each of the two 36-foot-wide fireplaces in the Great Hall rises two stories and required, according to Fred Seely, "120 tons of boul-ders to build." To warm guests on a chilly winter's eve, their oversized fireboxes were designed to burn eight-foot logs.

Based on historic photographs, the Palm Court was restored in 1991 to its original 1913 appearance (above left). Thirteen layers of paint covering a section of Arts and Crafts stencils applied to the parapet walls (above right) were meticulously removed. Mark Ellis-Bennett refurbished the stencils, and crews repainted the walls, restored the original oak planters, installed period-style carpets, and replaced the furniture castoffs with reproduction wicker rockers and settees more appropriate for the room (opposite).

The new Blue Ridge Dining Room (left) provides panoramic views of the Blue Ridge Mountains. Roycroft sideboards and lighting fixtures removed from the Grove Park Inn's original dining room (above) were combined with a new version of the resort's historic "G.P.I." chair. Plates, serving pieces, and even a delicate dessert set holding a coffee cup remain from the original banquet china and are displayed in the hotel (below).

J.B. #9.
Robinson.

A Castle Materialized

⇒ 1909-1913 ⇐

After a long mountain walk one evening, at the sunset hour, scarcely more than a year ago,
I sat down here to rest, and while almost entranced by the panorama of these encircling mountains
and a restful outlook upon green fields, the dream of an old-time inn came to me—an inn whose exterior,
and interior as well, should present a home-like and wholesome simplicity, whose hospitable doors
should ever be open wide, inviting the traveler to rest awhile, shut in from the busy world outside.

EDWIN W. GROVE
July 12, 1913

Edwin Wiley Grove, acknowledged as the "Father of Modern Asheville," was born on December 23, 1850, near Bolivar, Tennessee, sixty miles east of Memphis. His parents, James H. Grove and Elizabeth Jane Grove, lived on a small farm, which Edwin and his mother worked during the Civil War while his father fought for the Confederacy. After completing public school in Bolivar, Grove moved to Arkansas, where he reportedly studied pharmacy. In 1874, at the age of twenty-four, he arrived in Paris, Tennessee, eighty miles north of his birthplace, and took a job there in the local pharmacy owned by two of the town's most prominent citizens, Dr. Samuel H. Caldwell, a Civil War battlefield surgeon, and A. B. Mitchum, a local banker.

From the first days of his apprenticeship, Grove was determined to discover a formula that would set him apart from all other pharmacists. In just a few years the enterprising young man had persuaded the aging Dr. Caldwell and his partner to sell him their business, which in 1877 he renamed Grove's Pharmacy. "I had a little retail drug business in Paris, Tennessee," he later recalled, "just barely making a living, when I got up a real invention, tasteless quinine. As a poor man and a poor boy, I conceived the idea that whoever could produce a tasteless chill tonic, his fortune was made."

During the mid-nineteenth century, malaria stalked the South, killing thousands of men, women, and children in devastating outbreaks that left thousands more too weak to work. For centuries Indian tribes in the Andes Mountains of South America had known that

Opposite. In a 1913 Packard driven by Edwin W. Grove's son-in-law, Fred L. Seely, William Jennings Bryan and his wife (left, front and back) traveled to Asheville to visit the Seelys. Seated in the middle rear is Evelyn Grove Seely, Grove's daughter. The Arts and Crafts–style hotel, designed by Fred Seely, realized Grove's longtime dream.

Preceding pages. Workmen rushing to construct the Grove Park Inn pause at the end of a spring day in 1913 for a group photograph on the hotel's Sunset Terrace.

chewing the bark of the rare "fever tree"—the cinchona tree—could ward off the deadly disease, but it was not until 1820 that scientists in Europe and America confirmed that quinine powder, refined from cinchona bark, was an effective although bitter-tasting preventative for malaria.

Grove was keenly aware of the deadly swath that malaria cut through the wetlands; he was equally aware that most people found the taste of quinine powder, the only known protection against the disease, repulsive. By 1878, four years after he had arrived in Paris, he had developed his first formula for suspending quinine crystals in a liquid and making it relatively tasteless. Grove named his original compound Feberlin, but because of its high quinine level, it could be sold only by prescription. Continuing to experiment, he discovered that he could disguise the bitter taste of quinine by adding iron, sugar, lemon flavoring, and alcohol. The resulting nonprescription remedy, Grove's Tasteless Chill Tonic, was an overnight sensation.

Quinine, whether tasteless or not, could not cure someone afflicted with malaria, however. Once in the bloodstream, quinine hindered the growth of the malarial parasite, reducing the patient's fever and chills, but it did not destroy the actual parasite. To prevent an attack or recurrence, the label of Grove's Tasteless Chill Tonic advised people to take four tablespoons daily "for a period of eight weeks or during the entire malarial season." Considering the deadly threat posed by malaria and quinine's ability to at least control the parasite, it was little wonder that Grove's Pharmacy and his newly formed Paris Medicine Company (founded 1887, incor-

Above. Edwin W. Grove (1850–1927) was a familiar face to many Asheville residents. The famous inventor of Grove's Tasteless Chill Tonic spent the greater part of his summers after 1900 in the mountain city.

Opposite. The famous Grove pharmaceutical trademark was the face of a baby, which in this advertisement was placed on the body of a plump pig. The slogan "No Cure, No Pay" amounted to a money-back guarantee.

porated 1889) soon outgrew their Tennessee home, thanks to his "tasteless" formula.

In 1891 Grove closed his pharmacy and moved his business north to St. Louis, where a more sophisticated railway system, a larger manufacturing facility, and a growing sales force soon made his chill tonic a household staple. Even decades later, long after the threat of malaria had been reduced, Grove's tonic remained popular, for it was widely—although not accurately—advertised that it "restores energy and vitality by creating new, healthy blood." Regardless of the accuracy of his claims, in the late 1890s more bottles of Grove's Tasteless Chill Tonic were sold than were bottles of another recent southern invention, Coca-Cola. And at a time when a typical factory worker might earn ten dollars a week, Grove was well on his way to becoming a multimillionaire.

Although Grove had the Midas touch for the pharmaceutical business, his personal life was not as blessed. While still a clerk at the Paris pharmacy, he had met and married Mary Louisa Moore. Of their four children, only Evelyn, born in 1877, survived infancy, and Mary Grove herself died suddenly in 1884. Two years later, at the age of thirty-six, Grove married twenty-two-year-old Alice Gertrude Mathewson of Murray, Kentucky. Their son, Edwin W. Grove Jr., was born in 1890; their only daughter, Katherine, died of diphtheria at an early age after the family had moved to St. Louis. Grove himself struggled for extended periods with bronchitis and bouts of exhaustion, prompting his doctors to recommend that he spend a part of each year relaxing and recuperating in Asheville, North Carolina.

Keeping It in the Family

Savvy enough to realize that he could not build a business on just one product, Grove continued to use his St. Louis laboratories to develop new pharmaceutical compounds, several of which were variations of his famous formula. At a time when most medicines came in either a liquid or a powder form, he came up with an idea for the first cold tablet: Grove's Laxative Bromo Quinine. In 1898 his search for a manufacturing plant that could produce tablets for him took him to Detroit and the headquarters of the fledgling Parke, Davis and Company. It was there that Grove met Fred Seely, one of the company's most promising young managers.

Fred Loring Seely was born in Port Monmouth, New Jersey, on December 22, 1871, the son of Uriah and Nancy Hopping Seely. In 1887, after completing high school at the age of sixteen, Seely worked for eight years for Seabury and Johnson, a New York City pharmaceutical firm, and then for two years for the Frazier Tablet Company. In New York Seely also took a course in chemistry at the New York College of Pharmacy. He then moved to Detroit to work for Parke, Davis, where he distinguished himself by improving the design and efficiency of its machine for compressing tablets.

For one week Grove and Seely worked side by side in one of the Parke, Davis laboratories, perfecting Grove's formula so that it could be compressed into a pleasant-tasting cold tablet. In May 1898 Grove invited Seely to his summer home in Asheville. One week later, on his return to Detroit, Seely resigned his position at Parke, Davis, setting off a stream of accusations that he had stolen company formulas and plans for a tablet-pressing machine as well as a potential client—the Paris Medicine Company.

Seely's decision to leave Parke, Davis may have been prompted by more than just the opportunity to work with Grove. Several years later Grove recalled Seely's first visit to Asheville, where the tonic inventor introduced his new employee to his only daughter, Evelyn. Seely, according to Grove, arrived wearing "a Prince Albert coat and a silk hat and a white vest. He first met my daughter at this meeting, when he came dressed up, and it was only 48 hours before he became engaged to her."

Grove offered no objections to the engagement. In fact, he had been impressed with Seely's determination, leadership, and innovative flair, especially in the new field of tablet manufacturing. He also undoubtedly saw something of himself in the young man. Now forty-eight years old, he had over the course of a hectic twenty years transformed a small-town drugstore into a multi-million-dollar corporation. But the process had taken its toll: he had developed chronic insomnia and bronchitis. It appears, too, that Grove had begun to explore interests outside of the pharmaceutical world and may well have been looking for someone to take over the day-to-day operation of the Paris Medicine Company. Because his only son was just seven years old, Grove may well have envisioned Seely not only as his son-in-law but also as his heir apparent.

Seely officially began working for the Paris Medicine Company in St. Louis in June 1898, drawing a starting salary of thirty-five dollars a week, the same amount he had been making at Parke, Davis. That October he and Evelyn were married in St. Louis and moved to Asheville. Seely was placed in charge of his father-in-law's new subsidiary, the Tasteless Quinine Company. Its task was to perfect existing formulas and develop new products, especially in the growing field of tablet production.

In 1899 the forty-nine-year-old Grove suffered a relapse and was ordered by his doctor to remain in Asheville until his health improved. Convinced that he

Above. Fred L. Seely (1871–1942) helped create a cold tablet version of Edwin Grove's tonic. He married Grove's only daughter, Evelyn, in October 1898.

Opposite. Although he had no architectural experience, Fred Seely submitted this sketch of the proposed hotel to Grove in May 1912. The actual inn, completed little more than a year later, varied only slightly from Seely's original drawing.

could not trust any of his St. Louis employees to properly manage his company, Grove arranged for Seely to divide his time between the Asheville and St. Louis plants. Seely proved to be an effective and efficient manager and soon had the St. Louis factory running smoothly in Grove's absence. At that time the Paris Medicine Company was the world's largest consumer of quinine. In a move designed to sever its dependence on pharmaceutical distributors in the United States, Grove sent his daughter and his new son-in-law on a five-month, around-the-world trip to secure contracts with quinine plantations in Java, Ceylon, and India. "I think we felt nothing short of lonesome," Seely noted in his journal. "14,000 miles from home. Evelyn was the only American woman in Java and I believe there were [only] six or seven men on the Island who had been Americans at some time in their lives." Despite many setbacks and challenges, Seely negotiated a contract that secured for the Paris Medicine Company a steady supply of quinine for the next forty-two years.

On his return to St. Louis, Seely was rewarded by being named to the post of secretary-treasurer of the Paris Medicine Company at an annual salary of $2,500. With Grove still living in Asheville for the majority of the year, Seely continued to manage and improve the efficiency of the company's advertising and production departments. He was also granted a patent for a tablet-pressing machine, for which Grove paid him an annual royalty for its exclusive use from 1900 to 1922. With Seely spending most of his time in St. Louis, Grove decided that the Tasteless Quinine Company in Asheville should be merged with the parent company

Left. Hundreds of mules pulled wagons and sleds full of rocks and boulders down from the mountain to the road, where an "automobile train" waited.

Below. The only piece of motorized equipment used to carve the ledge on Sunset Mountain was a single steam shovel, which filled a steady stream of two-wheeled carts pulled by mules. The golf course and Kimberly Avenue can be seen in the background.

Opposite top. Grove's famous "automobile train," led by one of his three Packard trucks, could pull fifteen wagons of rocks containing more than forty tons of boulders.

Opposite bottom. While the stonemasons work above them, workmen prepare to pour the concrete floor for the inn's dining room. The workman in the center is standing where the north fireplace would later rise. Note the scaffolding, ramps, and forms used in the inn's construction.

and moved to St. Louis. By this time Seely's salary had increased to $5,000 a year.

The first signs of trouble between Grove and Seely began to surface in 1902. That October Seely suddenly offered his resignation as plant manager, citing health reasons for his decision to leave St. Louis. Although his dedication to the reorganization of the Paris Medicine Company had taken its toll on the thirty-one-year-old Seely, his decision might also have been influenced by Grove's total recovery and his subsequent decision that year to return to the company's helm. Rumors also circulated about tension between Grove's second wife, Gertrude, and her stepdaughter, Evelyn, who remained extremely close to her father his entire life.

When asked several years later what he had done at the Paris Medicine Company between 1899 and 1902, Seely replied, "I built the laboratory and equipped it, cleaning the business end of it up thoroughly, put it on a business basis, eliminated something like twenty traveling men, some of whom were drinking and neglecting their work, and I won't say I did it, but the sales and profits increased. . . . I got the business in such running order and left it in such running order that there have been very few changes made since." He added that Grove told him that "the business was now in such shape that he wanted the pleasure of handling it himself; that his health had improved and that he would like for me to leave the business and go to Atlanta to look after his property."

After a few months in Detroit, where Seely continued to perfect his tablet-pressing machine, he and his wife arrived in Atlanta in February 1903. There he supervised the development of Atkins Park, a residential development Grove had begun just east of the downtown area. Seely sold some of his shares of Paris Medicine Company stock for a profit of $15,000 and invested it in nine acres of land, on which he oversaw the construction of three rental houses. Within a few months, however, Seely had tired of the real estate business and announced his decision to move his family to Princeton, New Jersey, attend Princeton University, and prepare for a career in either law or education. Once at Princeton, however, Seely again changed his mind and, after conferring with

Left. J. Oscar Mills, who had worked for Grove on a construction project in Atlanta, came to Asheville to serve under Fred Seely as construction superintendent for the Grove Park Inn. In the summer of 1912, he and his family pose on the first pile of granite rocks brought to the hotel's site.

Opposite. Crates of red clay tile line the temporary ramp leading to the new hotel's south wing in the spring of 1913. Workers on the roof weave a web of steel rods in preparation for laying the concrete roof.

Left. The Asheville photographer John G. Robinson (1880–1921) documented construction of the inn with several dozen photographs. He crawled out onto the partially completed north wing on February 28, 1913, to capture carpenters building forms for the concrete roof. Each of the inn's concrete roofs was poured continuously to avoid any unnecessary seams. Large lights were installed to aid the men working on the roof at night.

Below. Italian stonemasons, some of whom had worked on Biltmore, the nearby Vanderbilt estate, apply stonework to the interior west wall of the Great Hall. The north fireplace was later built at the back right area seen in the photograph.

Grove, moved back to Atlanta to pursue other business opportunities there.

In 1906, without any formal training, education, or journalism experience, Seely announced that he and Grove planned to start a new daily newspaper, the *Atlanta Georgian*. The first issue came out in April of that year, and the paper grew rapidly under Seely's direction, but he struggled to lure regular advertisers away from the city's other two newspapers. During the second year Seely's editor left, so the young publisher himself began writing the paper's editorials. His exposé on corruption in the Atlanta mayor's office led to threats against his life and some national notoriety. As a result, in 1910 he was invited to introduce the perennial presidential candidate William Jennings Bryan at a talk in St. Louis, after which the two became lifelong friends. By 1911 Seely, who had grown discouraged with the newspaper business, learned that William Randolph Hearst was interested in obtaining one of the Atlanta newspapers. Grove, who had tired of underwriting the newspaper's mounting expenses—it had not yet shown a profit—concurred, and in February 1912 Grove and Seely sold the *Atlanta Georgian* to Hearst for $200,000.

For Asheville, Hotels or Sanitariums?

Before 1909 Grove's primary concern outside the Paris Medicine Company was the improvement and development of Atkins Park and other real estate ventures in Atlanta. He hired Oscar Mills to serve as his foreman, overseeing the laying out and grading of roads, installation of curbstones, and construction of granite pillars marking the development's entrance. Grove also instructed Mills to begin building a few rental houses on the property and went so far as to send Mills to Chicago in early 1909 to learn more about the design and construction of concrete houses, a skill that would prove more useful than either man anticipated.

While living in Asheville, Grove had also begun buying property, primarily timberland and pastures, on the city's northern outskirts. The success of Atkins Park in

Atlanta spurred him to expand his holdings and begin developing residential neighborhoods. Grove had watched as the publicity generated by George Vanderbilt's palatial summer home, Biltmore Estate, completed in 1895, as well as the subsequent expansion of the Southern Railroad system, had spurred interest in Asheville. Just a few years after establishing a summer residence in Asheville, Grove was prepared to take part in the city's growth and reap the benefits of his involvement. In 1904, even before selling his first lot, he created the E. W. Grove Park near the north end of Charlotte Street, complete with an existing one-story granite real estate office for the new E. W. Grove Park Company. As he had done in Atlanta, Grove named several of the new streets in his development for members of his family.

On October 28, 1909, Asheville's citizens opened their newspapers to learn that Grove had purchased a total of 408 acres of land east of Charlotte Street, including nearly all of the western slope of Sunset Mountain. Earlier he had purchased forty acres on the west side of Charlotte Street, on a portion of which he had developed his first residential neighborhood in Asheville—Grove Park. Included in Grove's plans, noted the newspaper, was a "counterweight railway from a point near the terminus of the Charlotte Street car line to the top of the mountain. He will also build an automobile road from Charlotte Street to the summit of the mountain, winding through his own lands; and will operate an automobile line from the Grove Park office over this road, through the park, for the accommodations of residents and others."

The reporter also observed that "Mr. Grove, it is well known, is abundantly capable to be able to carry out the gigantic plan of home building and beautifying to which he has by this outlay of $75,000 definitely committed himself. Asheville people have known him long enough to judge that he is not a capricious man, dreaming dreams overnight and forgetting them in the morning." No mention was made of any proposal to build a hotel on the site, although the writer noted that given the improvements Grove announced for his new property, "opportunities will naturally be greater for future development."

A month later, in a letter to Seely dated November 24, 1909, Grove commented: "I was almost forced to buy this property to protect my holdings there. If consumptive sanitariums had gone up on this mountain, it would have injured my property very much; now I am fully protected on all sides, and I regard it as a very profitable investment because Asheville cannot grow any other way. It has grown to the river, and no one wants to build in the other direction toward the depot."

Other investors had also been drawn to the opportunities emerging in Asheville, including the need for a large, modern hotel to supplement the thirty-year-old Battery Park Hotel. That fall a group of investors approached Grove with a proposal to build and operate a hotel on the peak of Sunset Mountain. Grove declined, stating that he was not yet ready to give up control over what he considered his most valuable piece of property in Asheville. "No part of the mountain is for sale," he wrote on January 31, 1911, "and if I should

sell any part of [it] for a hotel I would want a good price for it and in the next place I would want very strong restrictions placed on it so that I could always absolutely control its management [so] that no sick people would ever be taken."

For years Asheville's civic leaders and developers had wrestled with the dilemma of whether or not to promote the city as a destination for people suffering from tuberculosis and related respiratory infections. One faction supported the construction of public and private sanitariums; others feared that this would drive away tourists and potential homeowners. Grove's position was never in doubt: he strongly believed that Asheville's future as a tourist destination could be assured only if it were not also a haven for tuberculosis patients. He fought the idea of either public or private sanitariums in every way he could, including placing restrictions on any property he sold prohibiting the construction or operation of boarding houses and sanitariums.

An Inn Worthy of the Mountains

By the middle of 1911, Grove had embraced the idea of financing, building, and owning a hotel on the slope of Sunset Mountain. The previous year he and his son, Edwin, had vacationed in Yellowstone National Park in Wyoming, and in 1911 he sent his Asheville real estate agent, William Randolph, to Yellowstone to inspect the Old Faithful Inn (1904) and the new Canyon Hotel (1911). In a November 1 letter, Grove remarked to Randolph, "[I] am glad to know you are getting so much out of this trip from places of this kind [rustic hotels], which will be such a help to you in developing a hotel so different from anything in the mountains of North Carolina, and which will appeal to the people on account of the hotel and surroundings being so restful."

Seely had also begun to get involved with the hotel project by June 1911. That month he contacted Robert G. Reamer, architect of the Old Faithful Inn, asking for details and approximate costs of constructing the hotel and passing the information he received along to

Opposite. Chains, pulleys, and timbers were used to hoist the Grove Park Inn's massive boulders into place. This one was destined for the north fireplace in the Great Hall.

Above. Plush rocking chairs upholstered with red leather added to the restful environment of the Great Hall, first called the Big Room. Seely's inspirational mottoes were inscribed on the boulder walls and columns.

Right. The original stairs leading to the guest rooms, viewed from behind the front desk, were located across from the elevator. The lower flight of stairs was enclosed when the hotel's Sammons Wing was added in 1984.

Randolph and Grove. With encouragement from prominent townspeople in Asheville, Grove gave Randolph permission to solicit architectural sketches for a new hotel. As the real estate agent noted in a letter dated January 22, 1912, to an interested architect, "We want a picturesque building of simple lines, showing comfort all over, lighted and ventilated to the limit, to be attractive to the best tourist business, a hotel that will be home-like and not hotel like."

In their many letters, Grove and Randolph analyzed structural elements of nearly a dozen hotels across the country, but it was clear that the rustic hotels in Yellowstone had influenced them the most. On November 6, 1911, Randolph wrote to Grove: "We have the photographs and interiors [of the Old Faithful Inn] and regard them as the finest we have seen. We are glad to have material of this kind in view of the similar development you propose here."

Although Grove had photographs of the Old Faithful Inn and the Canyon Hotel to show the prospective architects, none was able to design a hotel that met his expectations. Beginning on February 26, 1912, each of the architects, including Asheville's own firm of Richard Sharp Smith and A. Heath Carrier, received the following notice: "The various hotel plans submitted do not meet with Mr. Grove's approval; he is not desirous of continuing the competition."

The architect who came the closet was Henry Ives Cobb of New York City, who wrote on April 5:

The scheme that I have in mind is to build the entire building of stone from the mountain, using the rougher boulders for the lower part and smaller stone as you go up. The variation of color and the light cement jointing will make a very attractive wall. I think the roof had best be of red if the rest of the building is of gray. We need not use a bright red, but get enough red into it to make the whole effect more cheerful. I also send you a rough sketch for the interior of the main room. In thinking it over, it seems to be the best results can be had by building it with stone walls inside, giving the rustic mountainous effect that you have in mind and at the same time being absolutely fireproof. [He also suggested that] very attractive columns could be made in the big lobby room out of boulders.

From Atlanta, as he finalized the sale of the *Atlanta Georgian* to Hearst, Seely began taking a greater interest in Grove's hotel project. In May 1912, after study-

Dated November 2, 1912, this photograph bears the caption, "The men who are building the Grove Park Inn, Asheville, N.C." Construction superintendent Oscar Mills can be seen below in the back row wearing a hat, gloves, and a buttoned overcoat.

ing several of the submitted sketches, Seely presented Grove with a sketch he had made of the proposed inn. A letter from Seely to a friend the following month explains what had happened: "We did not succeed in getting a satisfactory plan from any of the architects and for that reason I undertook it myself and, strangely, made a plan that suited Mr. Grove." Seely's sketch, a photograph of which has survived, reveals his debt to the Old Faithful Inn, but rather than constructing the inn of logs, as Grove had envisioned, Seely adopted Cobb's idea of using native boulders from Grove's surrounding land. Grasping the idea, Grove proposed that Seely take Oscar Mills and the Italian stonemasons who had worked on his Atlanta project "and under your direction build the hotel; [this] will be a great savings in money, as well as in the time required to complete it." As compensation for his efforts, Grove gave his son-in-law a salary of $7,500 per year and thirteen acres atop Sunset Mountain, where he could build a home for his wife and growing family.

Freed from the daily responsibilities of the newspaper, Seely rebounded with enthusiasm and energy. He and Grove carefully selected a site for the Grove Park Inn from the hundreds of acres in Grove's vast holdings. Halfway up the slope of Sunset Mountain and nearly 2,500 feet above sea level, the site would provide guests with a panoramic view of Asheville and the western rim of the Blue Ridge Mountains, yet, unlike a proposed site at the top of the mountain, would not put them at the mercy of the winter snows. Grove accurately calculated that being adjacent to the Asheville Country Club and one of the finest eighteen-hole golf courses in the South would only increase the attractiveness of his hotel. In May Grove and Seely walked the slope of Sunset Mountain and talked about their vision of the Grove Park Inn. As Seely later wrote, "The idea was to build a big home where every modern convenience could be had, but with all the old-fashioned qualities of genuineness with no sham ... all attempt at the bizarre, the tawdry and flashily foolish [would be] omitted."

It soon became apparent, however, that Seely and the architect Henry Ives Cobb would not be able to work together. Grove sided with Seely, noting, "We [will] both get more pleasure out of [the] hotel by building it our own way without interference of any architect." By mid-June, Seely and Grove had selected J. W. McKibbin of Atlanta as the hotel's architectural engineer responsible for transforming their ideas into blueprints and Mills as the construction superintendent. Seely, McKibbin, and Mills spent the month of June developing plans for the hotel, while Grove and his son, Edwin, ran the thriving Paris Medicine Company.

228-Loying Tile-Dining Room,
5-10-13. Robinson.

Building in "Homely Comforts"

With workers and growing piles of rocks and boulders only a few feet away, groundbreaking ceremonies took place on July 9, 1912, with Gertrude Grove turning the first shovelful of dirt. According to the *Asheville Citizen,* "The plans were worked out by F. L. Seely, who has recently moved here for permanent residence. Mr. Seely's plans follow the simple but strong lines of a period in English architecture that built for homely comforts." Seely had decided that it was imperative that the inn be open for the following summer season; much to the surprise of Grove and everyone else, he announced to reporters present at the groundbreaking that the hotel and its approximately 150 rooms would be ready for guests in less than twelve months.

From his wooden office perched on the construction site, Mills directed a crew of approximately four hundred men of various ages and races. Grove's wages were the best in the area: one dollar a day for a ten-hour shift, six days a week. Many of his workers had walked away from other projects to work on the hotel; in addition, Mills brought scores of laborers from Atlanta and erected a huge circus tent to temporarily house them. Aided only by a solitary steam shovel and scores of mules, the men set to work leveling the site, hauling countless tons of rocks and boulders from Grove's surrounding properties, and constructing wooden scaffolding supplied by Grove's nearby timber holdings and new sawmill.

Using mules, pryers, and ropes, the men collected granite stones, some weighing as much as ten thousand pounds, from land on several nearby mountains, including Sunset, Beaucatcher, and Black Mountains. Teams of mules dragged the boulders onto wooden sleds and pulled them down to the road. The stones were then hoisted into wagons supplied by a local Asheville business, T. S. Morrison and Company. Approximately fourteen wagons were strung together to form a train pulled to the site by one of three Packard trucks Seely had ordered to speed construction. This unique "automobile train" could haul forty tons of rock per trip and was featured in several national publications.

With one steam shovel and several mule-powered drags, the workers at the site cut a long ledge into Sunset Mountain for the foundation of the six-story structure. Italian stonemasons from Atlanta and Asheville, some of whom had worked on the Biltmore mansion twenty years earlier, carefully followed Seely's instructions, making sure that only the exposed, uncut side of each stone remained visible. As Seely later documented, "The men worked under instructions that when the Inn was finished not a piece of stone should be visible to the eye except it show the time-eaten face given to it by the thousands of years of sun and rain that had beaten upon it as it had lain on the mountain side. These great boulders were laid with the lichens and moss on them just as they were found."

As the stone walls rose in the fall sky, the carpenters constructed long wooden ramps for the men pushing wheelbarrows of rocks up to the stonemasons. Just six months after the groundbreaking, more than 1,200 lineal feet of granite walls, some more than four feet thick at the base and six stories tall, were nearly complete. Workers began pouring the concrete floor in the lobby while the stonemasons were completing the walls above them; when the time came to pour the upper floors, the men built a crude elevator designed to lift huge buckets of wet concrete up through the center of the building.

Seely and Grove had designed a roof that would be fireproof while also presenting the appearance of an English thatched roof. By February Oscar Mills, the construction foreman, was ready to start pouring the first of five separate concrete roofs that would cover the inn. The highest, over the Great Hall, represented one of the largest continuous-pour concrete roofs of its day. Atop the wooden forms, the men first wove a steel web of reinforcing rods a half inch in diameter. The square, twisted steel rods, some thirty-five feet long, intersected at six-inch intervals, horizontally as well as vertically. The rods added more than ninety thousand pounds of weight to the roof, supported by the massive granite walls and six concrete pillars extending through the main lobby and into the basement. Once the rods were in place, the men began pouring more than six inches of concrete over the forms in a continuous, round-the-clock operation. In a letter dated March 24, 1913, Mills wrote to his family in Georgia: "I had to come back to the hotel tonight. They are pouring the concrete roof on and are working sometimes all night. I came down off the roof and [have] taken these few minutes to write you all; the wind is blowing up on the roof like fury. I can see all over Asheville, but Good Lord how one peep of Dear Old Atlanta would stir the latent blood in my veins."

Once the concrete had cured, each of the roofs was

Opposite. Among John Robinson's photographs documenting the hotel's construction was this one of workers laying tile in the original dining room on May 10, 1913.

Right. The guest rooms were furnished with furniture from the White Furniture Company and lighting fixtures made by the Roycrofters. Many of the original furnishings are still in use today, although the footboards and burlap wallpaper have been removed.

sealed with five layers of hot asphalt and roofing felt and topped with a latticework of boards to which the men nailed red tile shingles, each approximately six inches wide, twelve inches long, and three-eighths inch thick, supplied by the Murray Roofing Company of Cloverport, Kentucky. To give the roof the desired English thatch-like appearance, the tiles were arranged in an irregular pattern around the dormers. "There will be no angles anywhere in the roof," noted a reporter. "There will be only lazy, graceful slopes and the effect will be something unique for this section of the country."

In March, as soon as the concrete roof was completed, workers began finishing the hotel's interior. Plumbers attached water pipes for the guest rooms to the three-foot-square concrete pillars in the lobby, after which the stonemasons covered them with granite. At either end of the 120-foot lobby rose the two massive fireplaces, inspired by the fireplace of Yellowstone's Old Faithful Inn. According to an early brochure, each of the 36-foot-wide fireplaces

required 120 tons of granite boulders to construct. The firebox in each is capable of burning twelve-foot logs atop the hammered-iron andirons that "weigh five hundred pounds apiece, and an average of twenty-four days' blacksmith work was done on each of them." A unique feature of the fireplaces is that the elevators are concealed within them. Seely reportedly designed the elevators within the huge fireplaces to remove them from sight and eliminate the noise they generated. He also housed the machinery in the basement, far away from guest rooms.

Turning to East Aurora

Several months before the inn's opening, Seely had contacted his good friend Elbert Hubbard, founder of the Roycroft Shops in East Aurora, New York, regarding furnishings. Seely had visited Hubbard at the Roycroft Inn several years earlier and, well aware of the high-quality furniture, lighting, and metalware pro-

duced in the Roycroft workshops, offered him the opportunity to provide furnishings for the Grove Park Inn. In characteristic style, Hubbard immediately announced to the readers of his monthly magazine:

The Grove Park Inn could never be complete in its fulfillment of purpose without the assistance of The Roycrofters. And so it is that the dining room will be entirely furnished with Roycroft furniture—plain, simple, straight-line pieces, genuinely handmade and with the quality the first and last endeavor. Too, from The Roycrofters' Copper Shop will come the lighting fixtures. These are also being made after special designs, with the loving marks of the hammer still on them. Nothing crude or impractical, but along the line of the most modern methods of illuminating, indirect lighting. Not an electric bulb will be seen.

For the opening banquet the Roycroft craftsmen furnished more than four hundred oak chairs, each bearing the Roycroft mark and the initials G.P.I. carved into the crest rail. In addition, they constructed six large corner servers and two massive sideboards for the dining room and a number of chairs, tables, and accessories for the offices, parlors, and billiard room, as well as the famous eight-foot-tall clock that originally greeted guests as they walked through the front doors. The Great Hall also featured large, comfortable wicker rocking chairs, straight chairs, and writing tables for guests, all produced by the Heywood-Wakefield Company. The gray tile floor was covered with handmade rugs imported from Aubusson, France, reportedly at a cost of more than $5,000.

In the short amount of time allowed, however, the small Roycroft furniture shop was unable to provide the more than twelve hundred beds, dressers, tables, and chairs required for all the guest rooms surrounding the Palm Court. On learning this, J. S. White of the White Furniture Company in Mebane, North Carolina, contacted Seely. As White later recalled,

Mr. Seely was a very exacting man and a hard worker and wanted everything perfect and did not believe that a furniture manufacturer in the South could make furniture satisfactory to them. After examining the sample, Mr. Seely was convinced that we could make the furniture, but had decided in the meantime that he wanted it made out of solid white oak and wanted to know if the samples could be delivered in ten days. We made the furniture and had it up there in ten days. It was absolutely satisfactory. Mr. Seely was so pleased with our work that he asked us to make many of the doors and other pieces used throughout the hotel.

The Roycroft Copper Shop, under the direction of Victor Toothaker, a well-known furniture and metal designer, did rise to the challenge of producing all the lighting for the Grove Park Inn. Each of the 150 guest rooms was outfitted with two, sometimes three, Roycroft

Today the inn's eastern facade appears much as it did in this 1920 photograph. The undulating roofline and granite boulders blend easily with the hotel's natural surroundings.

table lamps, as well as a copper ceiling light suspended on iron chains. All of the hallways and various public rooms featured Roycroft ceiling lights, including eight copper and mica chandeliers in the original dining room and twelve in the spacious lobby. Seely also commissioned the Roycroft Copper Shop to provide, in addition to the more than seven hundred lighting fixtures, approximately 2,500 hammered-copper drawer pulls to be installed on the bedroom tables and dressers manufactured by the White Furniture Company.

A Dream Realized

Work on the Grove Park Inn proceeded at a steady pace during the spring of 1913, but as Seely's self-imposed deadline of July 1 approached, it became apparent that the hotel was not going to be ready. Photographs taken the last week in June reveal that neither the main tile roof nor the tile floor in the lobby was complete. A nearby stack of furniture intended for the bedrooms may have indicated that they, too, were not yet ready for guests. Invitations bearing a revised Seely drawing depicting how the inn would appear after the landscaping had been completed were hastily prepared. Each one bore Grove's name and read in part:

On the night of Saturday, July 12th, we expect to hold our opening banquet—opening the Grove Park Inn to the public.

We have built what we believe we can honestly claim is the finest resort hotel in the world, and on that night we shall be honored by the presence of the Secretary of State, William Jennings Bryan, who will make the principal address.

I believe it is generally known that this enterprise was not born of purely commercial motives, but was the outgrowth of a movement set on foot by Mayor Rankin and a number of prominent business men of this section who finally called on me at Saint Louis and placed the matter before me. After deciding to act upon their suggestion I did what I could to build an hotel worthy of these wonderful mountains.

I sincerely trust, therefore, that you may be present at seven P.M., Saturday, July 12th, to view the building before the banquet, which is to be at eight o'clock.

A local newspaper reporter documented the opening ceremonies, noting that when the appointed hour arrived,

the four hundred guests were greeted by an army of gray-coated attendants. The great hostelry looked as if it had been completed for a year; not one person could realize that only two weeks ago chaos and disorder reigned on every side. While some portions of the hotel and the surrounding grounds have yet to receive the finishing touches, it stands today as it will stand for all time—a marvel of the builder's art, a triumph of architectural skill. There was no confusion in the reception or in the allotment of guests, and the elaborate menu was served with perfect precision. Seldom has a more representative gathering assembled in this immediate section. With a cabinet officer, senators, and congressmen, men high in the various professions, men whose total wealth would run up into the millions, last night's gathering was an auspicious one in every way, and will be long remembered.

Seely served as toastmaster at the elaborate, all-male dinner, after which he introduced each of the four speakers. Grove credited his son-in-law with the completion of the Grove Park Inn in little more than twelve months' time: "A man never grows too old to build castles and

Above. Secretary of State William Jennings Bryan was one of the great orators of the day. In his address marking the Grove Park Inn's opening, he proclaimed that Asheville's new hotel was "built for the ages."

Opposite. Four hundred of the most distinguished men of the South gathered in Asheville on Saturday night, July 12, 1913, for the banquet marking the official opening of the 150-room hostelry.

dream dreams. Standing here tonight in the midst of my friends and invited guests, I find a dream realized and a castle materialized. It affords me far more gratification than I can express in having in my immediate family an architect and builder who, by his artistic conception, by his untiring zeal, has studied out the very minutest detail, making my dream a reality indeed and accomplishing what, in so short a time, seems almost beyond human endurance."

It remained for Secretary of State Bryan to place the feat into historical perspective: "Today we stand in this wonderful hotel, not built for a few, but for the multitudes that will come and go. I congratulate these men. They have built for the ages." Mayor Thomas Rankin, nearly overshadowed by Bryan's presence, had nothing but praise for Edwin Grove:

By his brilliant fellowship, his broad enlightenment, and gracious hospitality, he has endeared himself to our population. In the great developments he has become a benefactor to Asheville. The successful completion of this handsome and magnificent structure not only now symbolizes the great public spirit of Dr. Grove, but it will be a monument to remind those who shall follow him of his foresight and accomplishment.

In the construction of the Grove Park Inn is to be found a natural beauty and art coupled with the ingenuity of man. This magnificent hotel typifies and embodies the acme of perfection in architectural design and is equipped with every convenience which lends to the comfort of its guests.

Here we see the triumph of architectural skill mingled with a scenic splendor of nature's handiwork, the whole blending in one great harmony never before equaled in the annals of the builders' craft.

BUILT FOR THE MULTITUDES

⇒ 1913-1927 ⇐

We are three and a half miles from the railroad. The street cars are not allowed to come near enough
to be heard. Automobiles are not allowed near the building during the night. Thus we have no smoke,
no dust, no train noise. We have pure air, common sense, digestible food, quiet in the bedrooms at
night, the finest orchestra outside of New York and Boston, a great organ, and an atmosphere where
refined people and busy business men with their families find great comfort and a good time.

FRED L. SEELY
1920

The first guests to arrive at the Grove Park Inn were greeted by William S. Kenney, the inn's general manager, personally selected by Fred Seely and hired away from the prestigious Mount Washington Hotel in Bretton Woods, New Hampshire. Seely had also recruited department heads of fine hotels from Miami to New York to Boston; the one exception was Asheville's Miss Gene Smith, whom Seely selected as the inn's first social director.

At the close of the opening night banquet on July 12, 1913, Edwin Grove returned to St. Louis, where he and his son, Edwin Grove Jr., now twenty-two, were making plans for an addition to their manufacturing facility. An advertisement that same year proclaimed that in 1912 the Paris Medicine Company had sold more than seven million boxes of Grove's Laxative Bromo Quinine tablets, now being touted as "The Original One Day Cold Cure." The cold tablets that had originally brought Grove and Seely together had permanently replaced the original Grove's Tasteless Chill Tonic as the firm's leading moneymaker.

Seely, however, apparently had no intention of returning to St. Louis or the Paris Medicine Company. He continued to arrive at the hotel each day, supervising the landscaping of the grounds, completion of the last of the 150 guest rooms, and selection of vendors for the hotel's supplies. In addition, he continued to oversee for Grove the development of the Grove Park neighborhood as well as construction of the 30,000-square-foot Overlook Castle, Seely's spacious retreat atop Sunset Mountain on the thirteen acres of land that Grove had given him and Evelyn on their arrival in Asheville. Construction of his

Opposite. Throughout the years, many guests came simply to relax in the comfortable rocking chairs on the Grove Park Inn's open terraces. Some visitors enjoying the early morning sun on the east terrace were photographed by John Robinson about 1913.

Preceding pages. Just a few years after the inn's opening, young pine trees planted by Fred Seely could be seen lining the driveway.

home, which Seely and the Atlanta architect J. W. McKibbin based on the Ford Castle in England, had begun early in 1913 but would not be completed until 1917. During that time Seely and his family, eventually numbering four children, lived first in a house owned by Grove and then moved into a suite of rooms at the Grove Park Inn, where Seely monitored every detail of the hotel's operation.

The forty-two-year-old Seely seemed uncertain what path he might take next. In a letter written just two days after the opening of the Grove Park Inn, his close friend Secretary of State William Jennings Bryan counseled him: "I have been thinking since I saw you of your future. You mentioned the ministry. Each of us must at his peril interpret for himself the call to duty, but I have been wondering whether it might not be worth your while to consider the starting of a school. You have the executive ability and the zeal. Dr. Grove has both the spiritual incentive and the monies." Before Seely could decide which direction his career would take, however, the assassination of Archduke Franz Ferdinand of Austria on June 28, 1914, altered the course of millions of lives. As America looked on, war erupted in Europe and continued to escalate, eventually locking England, France, Russia, and the United States in a deadly struggle against Germany and Austria-Hungary that would rob more than ten million young men of their lives.

After a promising first year of operation, during which Seely and Grove spent $27,000 in national advertising, the American economy faltered and room reservations at the Grove Park Inn failed to materialize; plans for a new wing with an additional one hundred rooms were put on hold. Dismayed by the hotel's losses, Grove wrote Seely on October 1: "We have got to reach some definite conclusion and stand by it and I am going to stand by our decision about closing on the fifteenth if conditions do not warrant remaining open. There is no use for us to deceive ourselves by thinking that the people are going to come because we are so anxious for them to come."

Austerity Rules

Grove released a statement to the press that the Grove Park Inn would close on October 15, but enough people arrived to keep the hotel open. Stung by what he perceived as Grove's lack of confidence in him, however, Seely began making plans to move to Washington, D.C., to take a position in the State Department under his friend Bryan. Grove had often been at odds with Seely over his management of both the *Atlanta Georgian* and the Grove Park Inn, but Grove recognized how difficult it would be to replace Seely and how much he would miss his own involvement in the lives of his only daughter and four grandchildren. Seely's decision to leave Asheville was made difficult, too, by his attachment to the city and the hotel he had built. "I shall leave Asheville with no little regret," he wrote his father-in-law on

Opposite. One of the first national advertisements for the Grove Park Inn appeared in the November 1913 *National Geographic.* The featured photograph was taken on the west terrace looking south, capturing the resort's famous rows of rocking chairs.

Above. Both horse-drawn and horseless carriages became a familiar sight at the Grove Park Inn during its early years.

Right. Guests arriving at the inn shortly after it opened in the summer of 1913 made their way down the same rock-lined road that hotel visitors still use today.

Grove Park Inn

November 1, 1914. "It is the most wonderful place to live and I am sure I will find my way back here in my old age if I am blessed with one.... The landscaping is finished," he went on, "the plantings are beautiful and the place is more beautiful it seems to me than any place I ever saw. Of course, you will grant me the privilege of feeling this way for it seems like a child to me."

Grove responded by giving his son-in-law the opportunity to lease and manage the Grove Park Inn. Seely leaped at the chance to run the hotel without interference and in a few weeks' time had prepared a formal lease. The term of the first lease Seely and Grove signed extended from January 1, 1915, to January 1, 1927. As first written, Grove was to have received 18 percent of all gross revenue for the first two years and 10 percent for the next ten years, but this initial lease never took effect. It was renegotiated on December 9, 1914, and replaced by a lease that reduced Grove's take to 8 percent of the gross receipts for the years 1915 and 1916

while maintaining the payment of 10 percent for the years 1917 through 1927. As the economy faltered, however, and the inn's revenues remained disappointing, Seely and Grove negotiated yet a third lease, which took effect on January 1, 1916, and was to remain in effect until January 1, 1928, further reducing the amount of money Grove would receive. Buoyed by profits approaching $1 million per year from the Paris Medicine Company, Grove waived his rental fee from the Grove Park Inn for the first year of the new lease and soon thereafter directed Seely to pay the rental fee directly to his daughter, Evelyn, to compensate her for money that her half-brother, Edwin, was receiving from the Paris Medicine Company. In addition, both Evelyn and Fred received generous quarterly dividends from the Paris Medicine Company for shares of stock they both had held since the first years of their marriage. Judging from the revisions in each of the three leases, it would appear that business did decline during the war years,

Opposite and above. The massive twin fire-places in the Great Hall appear today much as they did when the inn opened in 1913. The hammered-iron andirons were made in Asheville, but the wicker furniture was man-ufactured by the Heywood-Wakefield Company in Boston. The hammered-copper chandeliers came from the Roycroft Copper Shop in East Aurora, New York. Fine rugs imported from France provided a dash of color on the inn's original gray tile floor.

Right. The third-floor Palm Court, illumi-nated by a skylight more than forty feet above, has provided Grove Park guests with a quiet retreat since the inn's opening. "The center of the main building extends to the roof and is capped with an enormous sky-light which admits an ocean of sunlight," said Fred Seely in 1920, when this photo-graph was taken. "The effect is a most delightful sun-parlor to be enjoyed on cool days, as well as a sitting-room for evenings."

Above. On an elevator window shade, which could be pulled down when appropriate, Seely had this notice printed: "Please be quiet in going to your room—other guests may be asleep. No objections to remain in the Big Room as late as you like, but we greatly desire quiet in bedrooms and corridors from 10:30 P.M. to 8:00 A.M."

Opposite. Fred Seely had the walls of both the Grove Park Inn and Biltmore Industries inscribed with motivational bits of wisdom for the benefit of guests and staff. Similar aphorisms were a favored device of Arts and Crafts devotees such as Gustav Stickley and even Frank Lloyd Wright.

but Seely's skill and determination kept the inn open and operating without interruption.

In his customary style, Seely immediately set to work organizing, promoting, and managing the Grove Park Inn. Unable to work under Seely's close scrutiny and critical eye, William Kenney soon resigned as manager and was replaced by Paul E. Wilkes, who also left after working for Seely for only one year. From the first day of his reign, it was apparent that the Asheville resort would reflect Seely's personal philosophy.

Alcohol was not served, although Seely later permitted his guests to bring their own with them. Although Seely was a nonsmoker, oak-and-copper smoking stands made in the Roycroft Shops in East Aurora, New York, were placed in the Great Hall alongside hammered-copper spittoons. However, a 1922 brochure stated: "Ladies are requested not to smoke in the public rooms. We do not make this request with any inclination to be critical. It is simply a rule that has been observed ever since the Inn was built and we believe that it conforms to the feelings of the majority of our household." Four ladies' parlors, a writing room, and management offices were located on the first floor in the south wing. All were furnished with oak Arts and Crafts furniture, but the parlors also featured twenty-two-inch-tall copper Roycroft American Beauty vases designed to hold fresh flowers from the inn's gardens.

The Grove Park Inn's ability to remain open, if not always profitable, during the years leading up to and including America's involvement in World War I was due entirely to the unflagging efforts of Seely, who typically worked until midnight each night yet rose early enough to be sure that breakfast was served according to his instructions. In February 1915 he wrote to Grove: "We are getting simply wonderful results and are getting just the class of people we want to make a great success of this enterprise. They are old-fashioned businessmen, many of them, in fact, most of them, tired out, and some of them nervous with poor stomachs, and it takes all the time I can spare to listen to their praise of what they are receiving here."

To ensure peace and quiet at the hotel, all guests relaxing in the Great Hall were expected to speak in hushed tones. Seely ordered his staff to hand to those who were talking or laughing too loudly a printed card politely requesting that they be more subdued. At least one guest, Irwin Cobb, a well-known comedian, objected to this particular rule. On being handed one of Seely's cards, Cobb sat quietly for a moment, then removed his shoes, and, in an exaggerated motion, tiptoed to the front desk, where, in hushed tones, he requested his bill and left the hotel.

Seely remained adamant in his belief that the men who patronized the Grove Park Inn expected peace and quiet. A 1918 *New York Times* ad proclaimed, "If you are a Big Business Man and feel the need of rest after these years of strain, you should come to the Grove Park Inn, Asheville, N.C., where rest is made possible." Under Seely's rule, no automobiles were permitted to enter the grounds after 10:30 P.M. or before 9:00 A.M. Employees were instructed to wear rubber-soled shoes and report to their hall stations promptly at 8:00 each morning to be available for the guests but not to begin cleaning or making noise of any kind before 9:00. A sign in each elevator requested that guests not run water or make any unnecessary noise after 10:30 P.M.; for a time, in fact, Seely ordered his employees to turn off the water to the guest rooms after 10:30 P.M. to ensure that no one would be disturbed by any running water. As Seely explained in one of his brochures:

We must insist upon protecting the rights of guests who may have retired, and as the Inn was located purposely away from railroads, street cars and other outside annoyances, conversations, slamming of doors, throwing shoes on the floor and similar unnecessary noises are liable to annoy guests in adjoining rooms. We consider that our bedrooms are for rest after a reasonable hour, and we have the courage to enforce a discipline that makes rest possible.

To that same end, Seely also discouraged guests from bringing young children to the Grove Park Inn. "We entertain very few children," he wrote. "Not that we dislike children, but that we wish to maintain a place where tired busy people may get away from excitement and all annoyances and rest their nerves." At the same time he also insisted: "Positively no dogs of any size, value, color or ugliness [are] allowed at the Inn. Guests who attempt to smuggle them in in vanity boxes or suit cases will be asked to vacate their rooms. Sorry, but the Inn is for human beings who want to rest and recreate." Seely's efforts did not go unappreciated by his elite clientele. After spending six weeks at the Grove Park Inn in 1920, R. H. Borden, Canada's prime minister, wrote to Seely: "I have more than once expressed to you my appreciation of the fine purpose which you have in mind in the management of the Grove Park Inn. No lesson is more necessary or more worthy than that which teaches the self-centered to remember reasonable consideration of others."

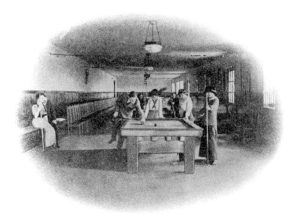

Despite his austere rules, Seely did make provisions for the entertainment, convenience, and recreation of his guests. On the inn's lower level he had designed a forty-foot indoor swimming pool and adjacent shower rooms, a three-lane bowling alley, a game room with a Brunswick-Collender billiard table and pool table, a pharmacy, and a barber shop, but, as he pointed out, the ceiling above these rooms consisted of twelve inches of solid concrete for absolute soundproofing. Seely also arranged for entertainment nearly every evening in the Great Hall, including string quartets, organists, vocalists, and lecturers. After each performance the staff would distribute Washington apples, along with a sheet of thin, gray paper for wrapping the core. When motion pictures grew popular, Seely had a large screen installed above the north fireplace, but, as he assured his guests: "We try always to secure plays and travel pictures and we take the trouble to censor every film carefully on a testing machine we have in a dark room in our general offices, before showing at our evening entertainment. This enables us to use many pictures that are excellent but would hardly be acceptable to us uncensored."

In 1919 Seely personally purchased a Skinner organ, "the masterpiece of the greatest organ builder the world has ever produced," and had it installed in the southwest corner of the Great Hall. The famed organ builder Ernest M. Skinner traveled by train from Boston to supervise the installation, which, according to a 1920 brochure, "required over sixty miles of wire for the electrical work. It requires a fifteen horse power motor to blow it and there are in the neighborhood of seven thousand pipes. It required three freight cars to bring it from the factory and four months to install it." For years afterward an organist provided guests with regular recitals, some of which were broadcast over a local radio station.

The Grove Park Inn menus reflected Seely's concern for the selection and preparation of high-quality, healthy foods. Fresh seafood was brought directly from

Opposite top. So that guests would not spill ink on the expensive rugs in the guest rooms, Seely requested that they use the Writing Room, located in a corner of the south wing. It featured oak Arts and Crafts furniture and tall copper American Beauty vases from Roycroft filled with flowers from the inn's garden.

Opposite center. A row of Roycroft "G.P.I." chairs lined the inn's three-lane bowling alley, located until 1930 in the recreation room directly beneath the west terrace. The space has since been remodeled into accounting department offices for staff.

Opposite bottom. For many years guests could enjoy a game of billiards in the same recreation room holding the bowling alley.

Right. The Grove Park Inn's original forty-foot swimming pool, located on the lower level, was removed in the early 1930s. Later used for meetings, the room is now an employee training classroom.

the coast; waiters served bread in the dining room from portable, heated warmers; and all the milk and cream came from the famous Biltmore Dairy on the Vanderbilt estate. Detailed descriptions of the source and means of preparation of each course were included on every menu, including advice for guests with chronic gastric problems: "Nearly everyone should eat fruit of some kind, and most people want it for breakfast. We supply the finest prunes packed anywhere in the world—they are preserved at the orchards in California and are not the usual dried prune. We serve them every morning year round." Guests planning to stay at the inn for an extended period were assigned a specific table and waiter for each of their meals; beginning with the second morning of their stay, a copy of their hometown newspaper would be on their table at breakfast.

Seely and Grove also secured an agreement with the directors of the Asheville Country Club for the hotel guests to be able to play its eighteen-hole golf course, redesigned in 1913 by Donald J. Ross, the renowned golf professional and golf course designer who had recently laid out the much-heralded second course at Pinehurst, North Carolina. The country club traced its origin to November 26, 1894, when a group of Asheville citizens formed the Swannanoa Country Club, also known as the Hunt Club (their primary activity during those earliest years was fox hunting in what is now West Asheville). The original clubhouse was located in downtown Asheville, just a few yards from the famed Battery Park Hotel. A crude five-hole golf course was laid out by one of the members in West Asheville in 1895 but was soon determined to be too distant for the members to enjoy. In February 1899 a new five-hole course was created by a member in a pasture at the end of Charlotte Street, and that year the organization was subsequently renamed the Swannanoa Golf and Country Club.

Left. Two chefs work in the original kitchen of the Grove Park Inn, where fresh foods meticulously prepared have always been a priority. Dairy products came from the Biltmore Dairy on George Vanderbilt's estate, while seafood was brought from the coast.

Below. The inn's original dining room was furnished with Roycroft chairs, to which arms were added by Biltmore Industries woodworkers sometime before 1920. When the room was remodeled into staff offices in 1988, the original Roycroft lighting fixtures were transferred to the Blue Ridge Dining Room in the new Vanderbilt Wing.

Opposite. Although women were not permitted to smoke in the Great Hall, no one kept them off the golf course of the adjacent Asheville Country Club. Edwin Grove and Fred Seely had entered into an agreement with the club to permit inn guests to play there. Overlooking the golf course, more than five hundred feet of open terraces ringed the rustic inn.

A few years later, citing the need for a larger golf course, the members formally changed their name to the Asheville Country Club and offered five hundred shares of stock at $50 each to finance the construction of a club-house and improvements to their fledgling nine-hole course. In 1910, aided by a gift of $25,000 from Grove and the Raoul family, owners of the nearby Manor Inn, the members hired the professional course architect Willie Park to design an additional nine holes. Three years later Ross was brought in to remodel the entire eighteen holes to create a championship-caliber golf course to be enjoyed by both members and guests at the Grove Park Inn. For decades afterward the inn, which owned approximately 230 shares of stock in the country club, contributed $2,000 per year toward the maintenance of the Asheville Country Club golf course.

Both Grove and Seely took steps to prevent potential guests from avoiding the Grove Park Inn simply because of Asheville's long association with tuberculosis sanitariums. Grove, in his characteristic manner, purchased a number of tuberculosis sanitariums and boarding houses and then demolished them; he also attached covenants to lots he sold preventing the building of any structures to be used to house or treat tuberculosis patients. In his advertisements and brochures, Seely emphasized that the "Grove Park Inn is not a sanitarium, a hospital, or a health resort. It is a resting place for tired people who are not sick, who want good food well-cooked and digestible, with luxurious, thorough sanitary surroundings." As a further precaution and assurance, the inn's water, which, like all of Asheville's water, was piped seventeen miles from the slopes of Mount Mitchell, was tested monthly and declared "as pure as nature ever produces." In addition, all silverware, glasses, and dishes were boiled not once but twice after each use. Even the coins used at the inn were washed in a special machine in the basement before being handed out to guests in change, and only crisp, new bills were issued to the front desk staff each morning.

Seely's work eventually paid off. As the nation slowly recovered from the wounds of World War I, the Grove Park Inn became one of the country's most popular vacation resorts for wealthy Americans. Most of the early guests came not for a few days of rest but for several weeks or even months. Many arrived by train, bringing with them their favorite riding horses as well as their personal staff. Many others, such as Henry Ford and Thomas Edison, traveled in caravans of touring cars. During the fall, reservations were required months in advance; new guests had to be approved by Seely before their reservations were accepted. The publicity generated by the regular arrival of notable guests—Presidents Woodrow Wilson, Calvin Coolidge, and Herbert Hoover; the entertainers Enrico Caruso, Harry Houdini, and Al Jolson; and the industrialists Henry Ford, Thomas Edison, and Harvey Firestone—helped spread the inn's fame.

Seely had previously met many of the inn's famous guests on one of his many trips or while serving as publisher of the *Atlanta Georgian*. He encountered Henry Ford when both were struggling to make their mark in Detroit in the 1890s; he and Evelyn first met Herbert and Lou Hoover in China in 1901, when all four barely escaped with their lives during the Boxer Rebellion; and he was introduced to Woodrow Wilson, then governor

A few of the most famous guests and luminaries to have stayed at the Grove Park Inn posed for this photograph in 1918: (left to right) Harvey Firestone Sr., Thomas A. Edison, Harvey Firestone Jr., a man who has been identified as Horatio Seymour, editor of the *New York World* (but who bears an uncanny resemblance to Edwin Grove), Henry Ford, and Fred Seely.

of New Jersey, at Princeton in 1912 and supported his successful presidential campaign. Seely took it on himself to personally entertain each of his famous guests, whether an established friend or a new acquaintance, by conducting a scenic auto tour of the area and a visit to Overlook Castle. According to an article that appeared in the *Asheville Citizen-Times* several years later, "Many a national figure was notified, on attempting to pay a bill at the Grove Park Inn, that he owed not a cent because the management was glad to have had him as its guest."

Jousting for Power

Managing the Grove Park Inn absorbed nearly all of Seely's time, but he still longed for a fresh challenge and, perhaps, the opportunity to step out from beneath the large shadow cast by his wealthy father-in-law. In April 1917 Seely purchased from Edith Vanderbilt a small but successful Arts and Crafts enterprise called the Biltmore Estate Industries. Begun in 1901 under the patronage of George and Edith Vanderbilt, two of Asheville's more recent residents, it had evolved from a club for teenage woodcarvers into a cottage industry of weavers and woodworkers. By 1917 Biltmore Estate Industries had outgrown its modest workshop and showroom in Biltmore Village, outside the famed Biltmore Estate. After the sudden death of her husband in 1914 following surgery for appendicitis, Edith Vanderbilt had neither the time nor the money to support and enlarge the small business. When Seely presented to her his proposal to construct a number of new workshops for the craftsmen on thirty acres of land adjacent to the Grove Park Inn, she accepted his offer of $10,000 for the business. Under Seely's supervision, the first of five buildings was completed that same year; by 1920, in addition to a team of woodworkers and woodcarvers, Biltmore Industries (Seely had immediately dropped the word "Estate" from the name) boasted a total of forty-five looms. The weavers produced what was considered some of the finest homespun fabric for suits and dresses in the world, eventually making Biltmore Indus-

tries as famous as its next-door neighbor and proving once again that Seely could organize, manage, and promote nearly any enterprise.

During the inn's early years, its owner Edwin Grove continued to enlarge the web of his financial empire, acquiring thousands of acres of land in Mexico, Texas, Arkansas, Tennessee, Missouri, West Virginia, Florida, the Carolinas, and Georgia. He also owned a cattle company, a lumber mill, a coal company, several stone quarries, a motor car company, and a real estate company. Under his direction the Paris Medicine Company continued to expand its cold-tablet distribution across the country and overseas. As Grove had anticipated, sales of his residential building lots on and around Sunset Mountain accelerated after the opening of the Grove Park Inn, motivating him to make additional investments in real estate around Asheville.

Grove continued to spend several months each year in Asheville, where local residents often saw him taking his customary walks. On an outing near the village of Swannanoa, twelve miles east of Asheville, he discovered an unusual deposit of stone, opening the door to yet another business, the Grove Gravel and Sand Company. A few miles away he initiated a new residential development and model community called Grovemont. One among the many stories told about him involved Thomas Wolfe. The encounter, which took place in 1922, was recalled by Wolfe's brother, Frank, and recorded by Alexander Turnbull in his biography of the famous Asheville author:

One day, when Wolfe was home for the summer from Harvard, he and a friend borrowed a car to take two girls to the top of Sunset Mountain, and driving through Grove Estate a tire went flat.

They had begun their unaccustomed struggle with the spare when an elderly man in tan dungarees emerged from the forest and offered his services. With his aid the job was quickly done, and Tom handed him a quarter which he accepted with a bow....

Some years later, Tom's brother heard the story from the man

himself; he was Grove, owner of the Grove Park Inn and the six thousand acres of Sunset Mountain. Frank asked if he had thought of returning the quarter, "No, I still have it," said Grove. "First, I kept it because it was the only tip I ever received, and then its preciousness grew in proportion to Tom's fame.

Despite the fact that under Seely's management the Grove Park Inn steadily grew more profitable for both Seely and Grove, relations between the two headstrong men soured in 1917. Disagreements reaching back to

their first days together in St. Louis and extending into the years when they mutually owned the *Atlanta Georgian* boiled over as they continued to disagree on how the Grove Park Inn should be managed, improved, and expanded. Further complicating their relationship was each man's jealousy over the other's relationship with Evelyn Grove Seely, Grove's only daughter and Seely's wife. By midyear the two men were barely speaking to each other. Their attorneys subsequently drew up another lease on the Grove Park Inn, further distancing their financial interests. That same year Seely resigned his position as secretary-treasurer of the Paris Medicine Company, a post he had held since 1901 but that had become largely ceremonial. His symbolic gesture came at a high price, however, for the company had paid him an annual salary of $5,000.

In 1920, in a move motivated at least partially by the conflict between the two men, Grove purchased the Albemarle Park Company, which included an English-style inn called The Manor and twenty large vacation cottages near the Grove Park Inn. Like the inn, The Manor catered to a wealthy clientele who stayed in Asheville for several weeks or months at a time; thus, the purchase virtually pitted Grove against Seely in a battle to see whose hostelry would be the most successful. The following year Grove also purchased the aging Battery Park Hotel in downtown Asheville and soon afterward announced plans to demolish the hotel, level the mountain across which it had sprawled since 1886, and construct in its place a fourteen-story brick hotel.

Both purchases were vehemently opposed by Seely, who claimed that they violated the terms of his lease with Grove. While the multimillionaire publicly claimed that neither The Manor nor the new Battery Park Hotel would compete with the Grove Park Inn, no one was convinced. Family members recalled that the seventy-two-year-old Grove had become increasingly jealous of his son-in-law's success at the inn and speculated that he may have wanted to remind Seely and the people of Asheville of the power and money he still controlled.

The twenty-three-year relationship between Grove

and Seely collapsed shortly thereafter when Grove announced that he had written a new will. The 4,500-word document provided explicit instructions for the disposition of his entire estate and personal belongings, down to his favorite watch. Conspicuous by its absence was any mention of the man who had once been like a son to him. In the document Grove even went so far as to state that the money and property his daughter, Evelyn Grove Seely, would receive after his death "shall be for her sole control and management and free from any rights, interest or claims whatever on the part of any husband or husbands, that she may at any time have." The depth of his split with Seely was evident in the stipulation that on Evelyn's death, her portion of the income generated by his trust was to pass directly to her children, not to her husband; in the event that none of her children was living at the time of her death, the will specified that the income she had been receiving from the trust was to be granted to Edwin W. Grove Jr., who was named executor of the trust and who was to retain the title of president of the Paris Medicine Company.

Grove made no attempt to conceal the contents of his new will from Seely. His plan to place all of his holdings—including the Grove Park Inn, the Paris Medicine Company, and hundreds of thousands of acres of land—into a trust rankled Seely, in no small part because the estate was to be managed by Edwin W. Grove Jr., who had never attempted to disguise his hatred for Seely. Although the annual income generated by the Grove trust was to be divided equally among Grove's wife, daughter, and son, Seely felt both morally and financially betrayed. Seely believed that in exchange for all he had done over the years to increase the value of Grove's investments—from the Paris Medicine Company to his land purchases in Atlanta and Asheville to the building and management of the Grove Park Inn—Grove had agreed, in Seely's words, "to transfer at his death a control in the medicine company to Mr. Seely, or if Mr. Seely should so elect, to transfer to him all other property owned by Mr. Grove, outside his holdings in the medicine company. Mr. Grove, it was set forth, agreed to do this because of long and difficult services rendered in his behalf by Mr. Seely."

Both privately and publicly, Grove denied ever having made this agreement with Seely. When attempts at a settlement stalled in December 1925, Seely filed a

Opposite. Edwin Grove and his second wife, Gertrude, maintained a home in St. Petersburg, Florida, where this photograph of the couple was taken about 1918.

Right. Edwin Grove (1850–1927) (at left) put his property into a trust to be managed on his death by his son (at right), Edwin W. Grove Jr. (1890–1934). In between them is grandson Edwin Grove III (1912–67).

Left. Installed in 1919, this Skinner organ provided musical entertainment for guests until 1927. That year, Fred Seely, who had personally purchased it, left the inn. The mahogany case was carved by his workers at Biltmore Industries. William Jennings Bryan made a gift of the animal heads after buying them during a visit to the West.

Below left. In 1917 Fred Seely purchased Biltmore Industries from Edith Vanderbilt of the Biltmore Estate and by 1928 had constructed, on land directly north of the Grove Park Inn, six buildings to serve his weavers and woodworkers. Although the looms are now silent, Biltmore Industries survives as an antique car museum, a history museum, and a thriving craft gallery.

Below right. Although Edwin Grove financed the Grove Park Inn, it was his son-in-law, Fred Seely (pictured in later years), who provided the vision and leadership that garnered the inn its success.

lawsuit against his father-in-law, attempting to force Grove to honor Seely's claim of an earlier agreement granting Seely, on Grove's death, the option of ownership of the Grove Park Inn. The suit, which involved an estimated $5 to $6 million in real estate, was still pending when, on January 27, 1927, the seventy-six-year-old Grove died of pneumonia in his suite atop the Battery Park Hotel in Asheville.

End of an Era

When the multimillionaire's will was officially filed the following week, it became painfully clear that Grove did not want Seely to be associated with the Grove Park Inn after his death. He assigned to William V. Curran, his private secretary and former secretary-treasurer of the Paris Medicine Company, the responsibility of "full control and management of all my real estate and other properties in the States of North Carolina, Georgia, and Florida" and declared that his investments in North Carolina, including the Grove Park Inn, are a "permanent investment and [I] desire that they not be put on the market and sold as a whole or in part." Shortly afterward Edwin Grove Jr. and Curran informed Seely that on the expiration of his lease on December 31, 1927, his services would no longer be needed at the Grove Park Inn.

Through his marriage to Grove's daughter, Seely was destined to receive access to a sizable portion of the estimated $10 million estate he had helped build. But Grove had instructed his executors to place the majority of his investments in a trust and dispense the income in equal amounts each quarter to his wife, his daughter, and his son. According to the will, on the death of his wife, Gertrude, Grove wanted the net annual income from all of the properties, investments, and businesses held in the Grove trust to be divided equally between Evelyn and Edwin. Only a few months after her husband's death, however, Gertrude Grove requested in cash the equivalent of one-third of the $10 million estate. Her request was submitted to the executor of her husband's estate (her son) and immediately approved. Less than a year

later, in 1928, Gertrude Grove died at the age of sixty-seven, but not before having willed the bulk of her personal estate, including an estimated $3 million recently drawn from her late husband's trust, to her only natural child, Edwin W. Grove Jr. In a letter written nearly twenty years later, Evelyn Grove Seely remarked, "As you remember, Mama Grove broke my father's will, but that was perfectly all right as I received far more than I deserved and I am certain that it was never intended for my children to have great wealth. It is far better for them to work and earn [and] possess sympathy with those who must balance the budget."

As his lease on the Grove Park Inn drew to a close, the fifty-six-year-old Seely prepared for yet another major change in his life. Anticipating such a day, perhaps, he had made the decision years earlier to keep Biltmore Industries beyond Grove's grasp. In 1927 Seely constructed three additional buildings for his craftsmen. That December he moved his office from the Grove Park Inn—to which he had dedicated sixteen years of his life—to Biltmore Industries, which became his sole business interest throughout the remainder of his life. One of his final duties was the disposition of the famous Skinner organ, which he had personally purchased and which had entertained thousands of his guests in the Great Hall. He had once considered moving the famous organ to Overlook Castle but eventually accepted an offer for it from the First Presbyterian Church in Baltimore, Maryland. The Skinner organ remained in that church until 1961, when it was dismantled and sold to an unidentified party.

The Grove Park Inn's first and most glamorous era ended in 1927 with Grove's death and Seely's departure. Although Grove had provided the land, money, and materials for the hotel that bore his name, Seely brought the philosophy, leadership, and vision that guided it to greatness. Neither man could have known that within months events would shake the financial footing of the entire world and threaten the very existence of the rustic inn that they both, in their own fashion, had worked so hard to build.

A STEADY COURSE
IN UNSTEADY TIMES

⇒ 1928-1954 ⇐

*It will be the policy of the new owners to promote a better friendship between the inn and
the people of this city and to give it a more important and active place in the life of the community.*

ISAAC "IKE" HALL
October 28, 1943

Fred Seely's departure from the Grove Park Inn on January 1, 1928, came at the worst possible time for the world-famous hotel. Rumors of an impending economic earthquake were already being whispered privately, despite public reassurances to the contrary from President Calvin Coolidge. From their St. Louis offices, the trustees of the $10 million Grove estate, Edwin Grove's son and William Curran, appointed Martin H. Burke as the inn's new general manager. It quickly became apparent that the trustees had no intention of honoring Grove's final request that his real estate empire in Asheville—including twelve hundred acres of land, the Grove Arcade, Battery Park Hotel, Albemarle Park Company, and Grove Park Inn—"be not put on the market and sold as a whole or in part."

On September 22, 1927, less than eight months after Grove's death and while three months still remained on Seely's lease, Edwin Grove Jr. and Curran announced their decision to sell the Grove Park Inn. By the spring of 1928, John S. Adams, an Asheville attorney who had been named commissioner of the sale, had found a buyer. On May 1, shortly before her death, Gertrude Grove endorsed the sale, justified, as the trustees claimed, since "it became necessary to sell portions of the real estate belonging to the said E. W. Grove ... for the purpose of making assets to pay debts." When no challengers came forward, the court approved the trustees' request to sell the inn. Although no listing of the estate's debts was required, the pharmaceutical and real estate empires that Grove had worked fifty-three years to build clearly stood on solid

Opposite. On September 10, 1936, President Franklin D. Roosevelt (hat in hand) left the inn to address a crowd of some twenty thousand persons at McCormick Field. To FDR's left is Robert M. Wells, mayor of Asheville, and J. C. B. Ehringhaus, governor of North Carolina. John Roosevelt, the president's son, is seated across from the three men.

Preceding pages. Sunset Mountain creates a bucolic backdrop in this 1920s view of the Grove Park Inn. In the foreground is the pine grove planted earlier by Fred Seely.

ground; the only apparent major debt the trustees had to settle was his widow's unprecedented request for one-third of the estimated $10 million trust in cash.

The lawsuit Seely had filed against Grove in 1925 was delayed by Grove's death in January 1927 but resumed a few months later as an action against Grove's estate. In his suit Seely claimed that a will and an attached contract written and signed by Grove in 1900 promised Seely on Grove's death the option of ownership of either the Paris Medicine Company or all of Grove's investments outside the pharmaceutical company, which in 1927 included the Grove Park Inn. The 1900 will and contract had both been presumed lost, pitting Seely's word against Grove's, but in a sudden and dramatic turn of events the lawyers for Grove's estate discovered the 1900 documents and introduced them on the final day of testimony. When read in open court, the will and contract clearly failed to support Fred Seely's claim, and the judge, without objection, immediately

dismissed his case against Grove and Grove's estate.

The same executors who had fought in December 1927 to have Grove's final will validated by dismissing Seely's lawsuit ignored Grove's final request not to sell the Grove Park Inn. Four months later it was bought by T. E. Hambleton and Donald McKnew, owners of a Baltimore-based brokerage firm, for approximately $1 million. On May 1, after receipt of a quitclaim deed from Gertrude Grove, the property was transferred from Hambleton and McKnew to the newly formed Grove Park Inn, Inc., "a corporation organized and existing under laws of Maryland and comprising Baltimore banking interests." The new owners shouldered a sizable debt: they borrowed $300,000 from the Continental Trust Company of Baltimore, to which they added $225,000 from undisclosed sources to pay the Grove estate $525,000. The balance of $475,000 took the form of a first mortgage with the St. Louis Union Trust Company, a co-trustee of the Grove estate.

Opposite. Rustic gates marked the Grove Park Inn's entrance until the 1970s, when they were deemed superfluous. The sign's first sentence reads, "Sightseers either on foot or in automobiles are requested not to go beyond these gates."

Above. The original stable, located northeast of the present Sports Center, was remodeled into an automobile garage in 1924 and later demolished.

Right. This small gas station, situated at the intersection northeast of the present Sports Center, serviced guests' and hotel vehicles until it was demolished. The photograph was taken around 1939.

Changing with the Times

The new owners made numerous changes in the Grove Park Inn over the next few years. Many of these alterations, undertaken to expand the hotel's clientele to include traveling businesspeople and corporate conventions, ran counter to the austere philosophy by which Seely had governed the inn and its guests for fourteen years. The Writing Room in the south wing was remodeled into the Card Room; two of the original four ladies' parlors adjacent to the Great Hall became meeting rooms; and a beauty parlor was added next to the barber shop on the lower level. The three-lane bowling alley on the west side of the lower level was torn out and the room renamed the Convention Hall, "available for meetings, dances or special parties," although the billiard and pool tables remained for several years.

One of the most radical changes was the remodeling of the original forty-foot indoor swimming pool (the new owners cited continual problems with the original design and construction). It became the Bath Department, with "expert technicians in charge [and] separate rooms for men and women." A 1935 brochure explained that "the Grove Park Inn Baths have been added to the equipment of Grove Park Inn in order that our guests may have the advantage of health-building facilities without the inconvenience and expense of hospital treatment."

Capitalizing on growing interest in golf, the management installed an outdoor miniature course opposite the east entrance, and the staff invented a game called "obstacle golf," designed to be played inside the Great Hall. In yet another move intended to attract families and children, the owners made two of the inn's most elite cottages, the Ann Hathaway Cottage and the Van Dyke Cottage, available "for families and special parties."

Although they considered Seely's methods of hotel management outdated, the new owners did not harbor toward him the same animosity that Edwin Grove Jr. and Curran had. Seely's Biltmore Industries next door maintained a news and gift stand in the Great Hall, where his staff also sold "the famous Biltmore Homespun, wood carving, bronze and silver novelties," including Roycroft products. A second shop in the Great Hall featured "hooked rugs, counterpanes, linens, linsey-woolsey, pottery, pewter, handmade furniture, hand wrought iron, mica lamp shades and other handmade products of this mountain region."

Presidents Come to Call

With his new office just a hundred yards away from the Grove Park Inn, Seely was a regular visitor and counselor to a succession of general managers who grew to depend on his advice in running the hotel. Seely evolved into a type of ambassador for Asheville: he often extended invitations to famous politicians and celebrities to stay at the Grove Park Inn and provided private tours for them to Overlook Castle and the surrounding area. President Herbert Hoover, a friend, stayed briefly at the hotel in 1930 and 1931 while in Asheville visiting his son, who was recu-

perating from tuberculosis at the Blue Briar Cottage on Sunset Mountain. William Howard Taft, former president and then chief justice of the United States, made plans to arrive at the inn on January 15, 1930, where "he hoped the balmy air which he expects to find in Asheville will in a few weeks restore his strength." According to the Seely family and the Asheville newspaper, Seely, as well as several other prominent residents, had offered Taft the use of his home and staff for as long as he wished, but Taft had declined, stating that it might seem inappropriate for the chief justice "to accept any favor which might obligate him to anyone." Even if Taft himself had been unaware of it, his staff undoubtedly knew that Seely's well-publicized lawsuit over his father-in-law's will was still pending in a St. Louis circuit court.

As president, Taft had tipped the scales at a much-publicized 320 pounds. When the seventy-three-year-old Republican arrived at the Grove Park Inn in 1930, he still weighed a robust 240 pounds, but his failing health restricted him to little more than a daily walk and a short ride in his custom-designed automobile. Despite the soothing Asheville climate and the efforts of Dr. Paul Ringer, his local physician, Taft's condition worsened. Sensing that death was imminent, he returned to Washington, D.C., in February, where he died of heart disease on March 8, 1930.

Despite the publicity generated by famous politicians, entertainers, and artists, the Grove Park Inn could not escape the repercussions of the stock market crash of 1929. The Great Depression paralyzed the nation, including the two groups of people on whom the Grove Park Inn had come to depend: the established wealthy class

Above. Chief Justice and former President William Howard Taft visited the Grove Park Inn in early 1930 in an unsuccessful attempt to improve his failing health.

Opposite. One of the inn's most elite cottages, the Ann Hathaway Cottage (known today as the Presidential Cottage) was built shortly after the original hotel to the exact specifications of the English cottage where William Shakespeare's wife was born.

and the growing business class. Without the leadership of a general manager of Seely's caliber, the inn faltered. On January 15, 1932, the Grove Park Inn, Inc., defaulted on both its first and second mortgages. Hoyle Sink, Buncombe County judge, appointed the First National Bank and Trust Company of Asheville as receiver for the resort, while the stockholders attempted to reorganize and refinance their two existing mortgages totaling $711,500. R. H. McDuffie, vice president of the First National Bank and Trust Company, supervised the inn during this period and appointed Albert N. Barnett as acting general manager. In October 1932 a holding company comprising second mortgage bondholders and Baltimore banking interests purchased the title to the hotel. George G. Shriver, one of the principal stockholders in the 1928 purchase, became president of the new corporation. Shriver announced that Albert Barnett, acting manager, was to become general manager, stating that "since the bank took over the property last January, an operating profit of more than $40,000 has been realized."

First Lady Eleanor Roosevelt, an enthusiast of handmade crafts in the Blue Ridge and Great Smoky Mountains, visited the Grove Park Inn in 1934 and 1937. Fred Seely played her gracious host both times, conducting tours of his Biltmore Industries.

Under Barnett's leadership the Grove Park Inn maintained a steady course for the remainder of the decade. Had the stockholders of the Grove Park Inn corporation not been saddled with a high pre-depression mortgage, the inn might well have operated smoothly despite the hardships of the thirties. As it was, Barnett came close to restoring the luster that Seely had originally provided. The two men became close friends, and in many ways Barnett attempted to emulate Seely's ideals and philosophy.

As both the country and the Grove Park Inn slowly regained their financial footing, wealthy guests and famous personalities began returning to Asheville. Among the most renowned were President Franklin D. Roo-

sevelt and Eleanor Roosevelt, although, true to form, their visits to North Carolina did not coincide. The first lady traveled by car through the Asheville region in July 1934 "in her quest for information on the hand-weaving crafts." She and her female traveling companions stayed at the Grove Park Inn, where they were greeted by Seely, who served as their host. After a morning swim in the pool at the Asheville Country Club, Mrs. Roosevelt was given a tour of Biltmore Industries. Seely then provided the people of Asheville an opportunity to see the nation's first lady by taking a pre-announced route through the city on their drive to Tryon, where they visited the famed Tryon Weavers and Tryon Toymakers.

Eleanor Roosevelt returned to Asheville and the Grove Park Inn in April 1937, while on a motor tour of North Carolina, Tennessee, and South Carolina. Like Edith Vanderbilt some forty years earlier, she took a great interest in the craftsmen and craftswomen of the Blue Ridge and Great Smoky Mountains, and, as in her previous visit, Seely served as her host and tour guide.

In 1933 President Roosevelt had signed a bill that provided $1.5 million for the development of the recently established Great Smoky Mountains National Park. Three years later he toured the mountains, arriving at the Grove Park Inn on the evening of September 10, 1936. Barnett, the general manager, had set aside fifty rooms for the president and his staff, which included sixteen Secret Service agents. The following day Asheville schools, stores, and businesses closed, and an estimated fifty thousand persons lined the streets from the Grove Park Inn to McCormick Field, where another twenty thousand had waited since 6:00 that morning to hear the president's midday address. Seated in his open limousine, which had been driven onto the baseball field and parked at home plate, Roosevelt delivered a brief but stirring tribute to the people and the region of Tennessee and North Carolina before continuing on his journey to Charlotte—and reelection.

The Great Fitzgerald

One of the most tragic figures ever to stay at the Grove Park Inn may well have been watching from his fourth-floor window as President Roosevelt's motorcade pulled away from the hotel that morning. The novelist F. Scott Fitzgerald, once crowned the chronicler of the Jazz Age, found himself and his novels out of tune during the depression years. In 1935, after doctors discovered a suspicious spot on his lung, Fitzgerald sought refuge in Asheville, where he hoped to revive his health and the literary brilliance that years earlier had produced *This Side of Paradise* (1920) and *The Great Gatsby* (1925). The thirty-nine-year-old author arrived in Asheville "sick, debt-ridden, and despairing." Only the generosity of friends and advances from his agent and publisher enabled him to live at the Grove Park Inn in rooms 441 and 443 during the summer of 1935. Faced with insurmountable debt and gnawing self-doubt, Fitzgerald could produce only a few mediocre short stories during his initial sojourn in Asheville.

After staying with friends in nearby Tryon for a few months, Fitzgerald returned to the Grove Park Inn in 1936. This time he was there to transfer his wife, Zelda, who for years had been hospitalized with advanced schizophrenia, to Highland Hospital in Asheville. Despite having Zelda nearby, Fitzgerald slipped into his old habits. Showing off during an outing to Beaver Lake, he severely dislocated his shoulder

Both the Grove Park Inn and the Jazz Age novelist F. Scott Fitzgerald fell on hard times during the late 1930s. Fitzgerald lived at the hotel during the summers of 1935 and 1936, when his wife, Zelda, was a patient at nearby Highland Hospital.

attempting a fifteen-foot dive and was confined for weeks in an uncomfortable cast. He tried unsuccessfully to dictate stories to a secretary, who recounted that "his usual pattern was to start out having pots of black coffee served to us at intervals, but as the morning progressed into afternoon and the pain and the stress increased, he would advance to stronger stuff. At the end of the session he would slump over, overcome by exhaustion and drink."

By the end of the summer of 1936, Fitzgerald was growing desperate. A young woman with whom he had been having an affair at the Grove Park Inn had returned to her husband. His manuscripts and pleas for advances were being met with rejection. Zelda's condition was deteriorating, and their visits together were tense and infrequent. On September 24, 1936, his fortieth birthday, Fitzgerald consented to an interview with a *New York Post* reporter; anticipating a favorable review of his long-awaited comeback, the author was soon devastated to read what was in essence his literary obituary. A few hours later he attempted suicide by swallowing a phial of morphine but was revived by his physician and a nurse.

Fitzgerald remained at the inn until that winter, when he moved to the home of friends in Tryon. In the spring of 1937, he journeyed to Hollywood, where he tried unsuccessfully to become a screenwriter. Although he appeared to be taking control of his life, the damage done by years of alcohol abuse could not be overcome. On December 21, 1940, the forty-four-year-old Fitzgerald suffered a fatal heart attack. Eight years later a fire destroyed Highland Hospital, killing seven patients trapped on the top floor. Zelda Fitzgerald, who was to be released the next week, was among the dead.

A New Clientele in Wartime

Although visits to the Grove Park Inn by public figures such as Franklin and Eleanor Roosevelt, entertainers such as Wiley Post and Will Rogers, and athletes such as Bill Tilden and Bobby Jones generated invaluable publicity for the Grove Park Inn, an increasing number of couples and families began taking short vacations at the resort. Typical of this growing clientele was a young couple from Kentucky who stayed for two nights in October 1936 on their honeymoon to Florida. Forty-five years later the woman wrote back: "What do I remember about the Grove Park Inn? The beautiful setting and grounds, our luxurious room, the elegant dining room, fine luscious silver, and service. In the elevator there was always a big basket of delicious apples! A silly thing to remember. I guess, however, it just seems one of all the many, even small, details the Inn provided for our comfort. It was indeed a 'Grand' hotel."

As war clouds hovered on the horizon, however, the Grove Park Inn struggled to remain profitable. In 1938 the corporate directors were forced to restructure their mortgage debt with the St. Louis Union Trust Company; two years later the corporation borrowed $100,000 from the Jefferson Standard Life Insurance Company of Greensboro, North Carolina, and instituted an ambitious although cosmetic remodeling program. The Francis Marion Room, earlier a part of the original dining room and now the hallway connecting the Vanderbilt Wing to the Great Hall, was remodeled to serve as the inn's cocktail lounge. Oak paddle-arm chairs and couches originally made by the Old Hickory Company were purchased from a lodge in Illinois to replace the lobby's aging wicker furniture. The

The humorist Will Rogers, a celebrated guest of the Grove Park Inn, appeared in the Ziegfeld Follies and a number of motion pictures. He was also the author of a popular column in the *New York Times*.

owners also thought that the Great Hall needed more light, but rather than supplementing the original twelve solid-copper Roycroft chandeliers, workers removed and discarded their rounded, copper pans and replaced them with flat, frosted-glass panels. As the crowning touch to their disfigurement, four medieval fleurs-de-lis were attached to each chandelier in an attempt to duplicate the interior of a European castle.

Additional plans for the inn were set aside in December 1941, when Congress declared war on the Axis powers of Germany, Italy, Hungary, and Japan. The U.S. government quickly arrested hundreds of Axis diplomats and their families who had been living in the United States, most in Washington, D.C. The plan was to keep them as safe and secure as the government hoped its own emissaries overseas would be treated by the nation's new enemies. Several hundred diplomats were interned at the Homestead Hotel in Hot Springs, Virginia, and the Greenbrier Hotel in White Sulphur Springs, West Virginia. When it became apparent that additional housing would be required, agents from the Federal Bureau of Investigation inspected the Grove Park Inn, declaring it and its staff suitable for their needs.

The terms of the agreement between the government and the hotel were simple: in return for providing rooms and meals for the diplomats and their families, the inn's owners would be guaranteed $8 a day for adults and $5 a day for children for a minimum of 225 persons. According to a story in the *Asheville Times*, the diplomats would pay for their accommodations from foreign bank accounts frozen and controlled by the federal government. During the time the government leased the hotel, the Grove Park Inn would not be allowed to accept outside guests.

On April 3, 1942, with no prior public announcement, two trains arrived in Asheville with 242 Italian, Hungarian, and Bulgarian diplomats, their families, and, in many cases, their private staffs. As a reporter noted, it seemed evident from their clothing, luggage, and servants that the new guests at the Grove Park Inn were accustomed to luxurious surroundings. Approximately forty-eight local men were hired to guard the nineteen-acre grounds. The area they patrolled was not delineated by barbed wire, but extra lights had been installed and the guards were armed. The diplomatic families were permitted to roam the grounds freely, making use of the same facilities that hotel guests had used during peacetime—with the exception of the Asheville Country Club golf course.

As expected, the government had begun negotiating an exchange of diplomats with the Axis powers even before the diplomats and their families arrived at the Grove Park Inn. Most of the new guests were quietly transported out of Asheville on May 5, 1942, but less than two weeks later were replaced by sixty-three Japanese and 155 Germans, none of whom were ranking diplomats, and their families. Security was tightened for this second group of internees, a reflection of their perceived threat or of the scars already left by the terrible war. By the middle of June, all but twenty-three of the Axis diplomats and nationals had been transferred from the inn in preparation for their journey home; those who remained had requested to live in the United States and were soon transported to appropriate locations.

From his office at Biltmore Industries, Seely had watched with great concern as the new owners, the depression, and the war took its toll on the Grove Park Inn. On the morning of March 14, 1942, at the age of

Bobby Jones, the first player to win open golf championships in both the United States and Great Britain (1930), tries out Asheville Country Club's eighteen-hole golf course adjacent to the Grove Park Inn.

seventy, he died in his sleep at Overlook Castle. Several hundred citizens paid their last respects there to a man the *Citizen-Times* called "A City-Builder." The people of Asheville mourned the loss of one of their leading businessmen and wealthiest residents with no less sympathy and appreciation than they had shown on the death of his father-in-law fifteen years earlier. In his obituary Seely was praised for having persuaded the American Enka Corporation to establish its plant in Asheville, for having donated to local charities "the equivalent of several sizable fortunes," and for having dedicated thirty years of his life to the welfare of the city in which he had lived since his arrival in 1912. In another ironic turn of events, Seely's last years had been spent renovating the Battery Park Hotel, which he and Evelyn had been deeded in 1940 by the St. Louis Union Trust Company as part of a settlement involving the Grove estate.

In the summer of 1942, the Grove Park Inn staff set to work preparing the resort for its summer trade, but even before the departure of the last of the Axis diplomats came confirmation that the U.S. Navy intended to lease the hotel beginning in October. The goal was to use the inn as a "rest and recreation center ... to prevent casualties, particularly nervous casualties," but it became necessary to temporarily house wounded seamen while the Appalachian Hall on the old Kenilworth Inn property was being transformed into a military convalescent center. Under the direction of Lieutenant-Commander J. B. Sutherland, the inn's staff and general manager, Burton S. Frei, greeted the first group of naval aviation officers and wounded seamen, whose stays would range from a few days to several weeks. Once again, guards patrolled the grounds of the Grove Park Inn, but this time their primary duty was to prevent curious citizens from disturbing the new guests.

The navy relinquished control of the Grove Park Inn on June 1, 1943. Not long afterward, the St. Louis Union Trust Company—which, as the original first mortgage holder, had been forced to foreclose on the property before the war—sought a buyer for the 150-room hotel. On October 27, 1943, it was announced that Isaac "Ike" Hall, an Oklahoma City businessman who had made his fortune in oil and real estate developments, had purchased the inn. Although the price was not officially disclosed, Hall reportedly paid $230,000 for the thirty-year-old hotel.

The following spring Hall and the Grove Park Inn basked in the glow of publicity surrounding the announcement that Manuel L. Quezon, the Philippine president-in-exile, had selected the resort for a month-long period of rest and relaxation. He and his family had barely escaped Japanese invaders in 1942 and, at the invitation of President Roosevelt, had established the headquarters of the Philippine government in Washington, D.C. President Quezon, his family, and his private staff, who had spent the winter of 1943 in Miami, arrived at the Grove Park Inn on April 19, 1944, where they established temporary government headquarters in the Ann Hathaway Cottage (now known as the Presidential Cottage). Quezon, who suffered from a respiratory disease, was transported from the railway station to the Grove Park Inn by ambulance. He and a small staff officially operated their government-in-exile from the Grove Park Inn until mid-June, when they returned to Washington to await the end of the war.

The Government Returns

Asheville citizens awoke on Sunday morning, July 23, 1944, to a double-banner headline in the *Citizen-Times* announcing the federal government's decision to turn Asheville's four largest hotels into redistribution centers for returning combat soldiers. As the newspaper reported: "Asheville was chosen as the site for the cen-

ter to serve the Southeast because of its splendid year-around climate and because it is one of the outstanding and most beautiful resort cities in Eastern America. The center will be one of more than a score throughout the nation." The four hotels were the George Vanderbilt, Asheville-Biltmore, Battery Park, and Grove Park Inn. The redistribution centers were to provide a relaxing atmosphere for soldiers of the army ground forces, including infantry, artillery, and armored units, who had spent a minimum of forty-five days in combat duty. Most of these men and women had not seen their families since first entering the military service. All personnel, the army emphasized, would be "physically and mentally well."

Qualifying soldiers first received a twenty-one-day furlough to visit their homes and then were ordered to report to one of the redistribution centers for ten to fourteen days for physical examinations, paperwork, back pay, and reassignment to noncombat duty. They were allowed to bring their spouses with them to Asheville, where they could use the complete facilities of the Asheville Country Club. Most of the officers assigned to Asheville beginning in September 1944 were housed at the Grove Park Inn, as were the majority of the soldiers accompanied by spouses. In writing about the inn, the *Citizen-Times* observed that

in recent years it has been operated much more on the general hotel pattern, with conventions not infrequently held there, but the Grove Park Inn still caters to the better class. The Inn, in addition to providing the finest of accommodations, will continue to operate the riding stables, skeet range, miniature golf, tennis courts and other recreational facilities on its grounds and will also handle the contracts of the Asheville Golf and Country Club course privileges for the soldiers and their wives desiring to play golf.

Although Asheville was justifiably proud of its patriotic spirit, not everyone was pleased with the manner in which "the representatives of the War Department came and saw and took." In an editorial that followed the announcement in the *Citizen-Times*, the newspaper pointed

Right. The inn's first cocktail lounge was located by 1935 in what is now the Vanderbilt Wing connector. Formerly called the Francis Marion Room, it remained a cocktail lounge until the arrival of the Jack Tar Hotels management in 1955.

Below. By the early 1940s the wicker furniture in the Great Hall had been replaced by oak paddle-arm sofas and chairs. Although the Roycroft chandeliers had been altered by this time, the stone columns remained intact. The gift shop is at the far right.

out that the influx of hundreds of military personnel would "strain to the breaking point our already overtaxed housing, eating and transportation facilities" as well as close the city's doors to the tourist trade on which it had grown to depend. Hundreds of guests in the city's four largest hotels were asked to vacate their rooms, and hundreds more were notified that their reservations had been canceled. While the staffs at the hotels, including the Grove Park Inn, remained intact, many of the businesses and shops located within them were forced to close.

For Hall, the inn's new owner, the arrival of the military in 1944 was a stroke of financial good fortune, however. With no experience and little interest in hotel management, Hall had neither the background nor the incentive to compete with the growing number of Asheville hotels catering to tourists, conventions, wealthy vacationers, and public officials. The contract with the U.S. government, which kept the Grove Park

Inn filled with officers, enlisted men, and their wives through the war's end in September 1945, reportedly paid Hall more than $100,000 per year and also stipulated that the government had to refurbish the hotel in preparation for its return to civilian use.

In 1946, as the nation adjusted to life after the war, Hall leased the inn to the Abraham Sonnabend corporate interests. Operating the hotel under its general manager, H. L. Thomas, the company made no major changes or improvements. The owners did attempt to maintain the inn's former image, advertising in 1949 that it has "an excellent orchestra which plays during luncheons, dinner and for dancing each evening," For the first time, however, the Grove Park Inn was closed during the winter, opening only from April until early November from 1946 through 1951.

The military returned one final time, although in a far less disruptive manner. On April 13, 1947, General

Dwight D. Eisenhower, then army chief of staff, and his wife, Mamie, arrived at the Grove Park Inn for an overnight stay. Eisenhower had just completed a fourteen-day inspection tour of army installations in several southern states and remained in virtual seclusion during his brief visit to the hotel. It was not until after the military entourage had departed that the general manager confirmed that the general and his wife had stayed at the Ann Hathaway Cottage.

Before the war and after, the Asheville Country Club golf course below the Grove Park Inn remained a favorite, serving as a stop on the Professional Golf Association tour from 1933 until 1951. Even such notable golfers as Ben Hogan and Sam Snead had to supplement their tour winnings with exhibition matches, however, and it was not unusual for the people of Asheville to read an announcement in the newspaper or spot a poster in the local drugstore about an exhibition of professional golfers to be held on the course. As one golf historian noted: "They had rare and wonderful moments out here barnstorming in the 1940's and fifties. They'd put up flyers around town and charge people fifty cents to watch. They'd gamble with the local big shots in town for three or four days to cover their rooms and bar tabs, then go on to the next stop."

In the years following the war and the departure of the Sonnabend management, which had leased the Grove Park Inn from 1946 until 1950, the inn depended solely on its reputation as a fine hostelry: as its fortieth birthday approached, the owner neither promoted nor improved the aging structure. Hall, described by many as a "big, rough cowboy," managed the inn from his office in the Great Hall or from the Ann Hathaway Cottage, where he

Above. The visit of General Dwight D. Eisenhower and his wife, Mamie, on April 13, 1947, was kept secret until after the couple had left the hotel the following day.

Opposite. Wartime romances blossomed on the Grove Park's terraces with the arrival in Asheville of naval officers in 1942 and 1943.

and his family lived. Unable to get along with any of his managers, Hall attempted to run the inn himself, opening it year-round beginning in 1952. According to his former employees, however, he never seemed happy at the hotel. He began attempting to sell it as soon as the Sonnabend Corporation departed, but his asking price and the inn's deteriorating condition frightened off any potential investors. Despite his personal unhappiness, Hall sponsored "Dollar Dances" at the Grove Park Inn every Saturday night, charging only one dollar for anyone who wanted to come to enjoy the music and dance.

As the country and Asheville adjusted to a new decade and a changing postwar era, the Grove Park Inn struggled to survive. Much of what had made it great—modern facilities, solid management, and a reputation for fine service—had eroded since Edwin Grove's death and Fred Seeley's departure two decades earlier. Although the hotel's granite walls appeared impervious to age, little had been done to update or maintain the water, plumbing, and electrical lines within them. The oak Arts and Crafts furniture, French rugs, and imported linens, which a half century earlier had been the best that money could buy, now were worn, soiled, and stained. Neither old enough to be considered quaint nor new enough to be called modern, the Grove Park Inn was no longer the pride of Asheville. A growing number of conventions, tourists, entertainers, and politicians were opting to stay elsewhere. Local merchants watched nervously as the inn's unpaid bills accumulated; most began demanding cash before making a delivery. By 1954 it seemed that Hall might never find a buyer, and the hotel's fate remained uncertain. The Grove Park Inn, many predicted, would soon close its doors forever.

Making It Modern

I was entranced with the idea of the thing, the uniqueness of the big, uncut stones, and one unusual touch—
a big bowl of apples in the lobby for the guests. But I bought it primarily because we liked Asheville so much.

CHARLES A. SAMMONS
April 29, 1984

On August 10, 1955, Ed Leach, president of the Jack Tar Hotels Corporation in Dallas, flew to Asheville to bid on the Battery Park Hotel, which was being sold by Edwin Grove's heirs. That noon Leach left the courthouse where the sale was being conducted, rented a car, and drove out to see the Grove Park Inn, which he had heard about but never seen. As he turned off Macon Avenue and drove down the stone-lined drive leading to the entrance, Leach noticed a rather bedraggled man, dressed in an old pair of dungarees and an undershirt and sitting with a bottle of bourbon in his hand on the front steps of the Ann Hathaway Cottage.

Leach parked in the deserted lot and then walked into the cavernous Great Hall, which, except for a very dignified bellman, was nearly empty. "The place was gloomy," he recalled, "The drapes were dusty, the furniture old. It didn't look like a thing had been done to it since 1913. I walked around, had a meager lunch in the dining room, and, like any good hotel man, started asking questions. When the old bellman let it be known that the place was for sale, I asked, 'Where's the owner?'" Pointing out the door, he replied, "Up there, sittin' out front of his cottage."

It did not take Leach long to figure out that Ike Hall was an unhappy man. He had owned the Grove Park Inn since 1944 but for five years had been trying to find a buyer for the old hotel. His wife had already moved back to Oklahoma with their two young girls, one of whom suffered from asthma, and Hall was anxious to join

Opposite. The opening of the cloverleaf-shaped pool in 1956 and the Fairway Lodge (out of view) in 1958 signaled the beginning of a new era for the Grove Park Inn.

Preceding pages. The Fairway Lodge was built southwest of the original main building and offered guests a panoramic view of the eighteen-hole golf course. Although it proved popular in 1958, the Fairway Lodge soon became outdated. It was demolished in 1982 to make way for the Grove Park's more harmonious and much larger Sammons Wing.

them. That afternoon Hall drove Leach around the hotel grounds and introduced him to Harry Blomberg, an Asheville businessman who had purchased and saved Biltmore Industries in 1953. "If the right kind of people got ahold of that old hotel," Blomberg told Leach, "it could make money."

Later that afternoon Leach phoned his boss, Charles A. Sammons, in Dallas. "Charlie," he said, "you have got to come up here." Sammons trusted Ed Leach's judgment, but he did not rush to Asheville to meet Hall: in addition to being a shrewd businessman, he already knew about the Grove Park Inn. Born on June 5, 1898, in Ardmore, Oklahoma, Sammons was sent with his two sisters to live with an aunt in Plano, Texas, in 1909 following the deaths of their parents. After graduating from high school, the enterprising Sammons started his first business—buying and selling carloads of hay and grain. He quickly established a solid reputation and a line of credit with the Security National Bank, even though he was not yet of legal age.

Charles A. Sammons (1898–1988) of Dallas purchased the Grove Park Inn from Ike Hall in 1955 and immediately set out to renovate the ailing forty-two-year-old hotel.

Sammons soon expanded both his knowledge and his business, taking courses in bookkeeping and business law and then branching out into cotton speculation. By 1928, at the age of thirty-one, Sammons had accumulated sizable savings. These, along with the bank, were wiped out by the Great Depression.

Undaunted, the young entrepreneur and his new bride, Rosine, moved to Waco, where he began rebuilding his finances in the cotton business. There he met two men who had experience in the insurance field but who, like himself, had been set back by the depression. The three formed the Postal Indemnity Company, an insurance business they soon moved to Dallas. While his two partners built the sales force, Sammons took charge of the young company's organization. Years later he remarked that he had made his fortune in the insurance business but had never sold a single policy. "I guess the closest thing I did to selling was to convince a few Dallas banks to lend me money when I needed it."

Under Sammons's direction, the company quickly expanded its territory and acquired other mutual insurance businesses, several in states other than Texas. By 1938, however, the partnership had dissolved; after the death of one partner, the other moved to Indiana to run one of the insurance companies the three had acquired there. Sammons remained in Texas, where that year he founded the Reserve Life Insurance Company and then built an accident and health insurance branch that grew quickly during the war era. Following a heart attack in 1948, Sammons rebounded with characteristic energy. As the nation settled into the 1950s Sammons, not unlike Edwin Grove some forty years earlier, was ready to expand his financial empire into new fields.

When Sammons learned, in the early 1950s, that the eighty-five-room Jack Tar Hotel in Galveston, Texas, was for sale, he decided to buy it, in part because he, his wife, and his daughter, Mary Ann, had often stayed there. Sammons enjoyed the challenges presented by the hotel business and within a few years had purchased or constructed hotels in Charleston, South Carolina; Marathon and Clearwater, Florida; and Orange, Texas. Leach, the former manager of the original Jack Tar Hotel in Galveston, quickly became Sammons's close friend, trusted employee, and president of the rapidly growing Jack Tar Hotels Corporation. As Leach explained: "Charlie Sammons loved to set up companies and then make someone president. He had nearly a dozen at one time, just like me, but he always made it a point to keep in touch with all of his projects."

One month after touring the Grove Park Inn, Leach arranged a Sunday morning meeting in Dallas between Sammons and Hall. Although anxious to sell the aging inn, Hall was convinced that it was worth $650,000. Sammons, pointing out that the hotel had only 150 guest rooms, thirty-five without a private bath, offered Hall $400,000. By noon, when Hall had to leave for the airport, the asking price was down to $500,000, but Sammons remained adamant. After it became apparent that the two men could not reach an agreement, Leach offered to drive Hall to the airport. In the men's room, he made one final pitch. "Ike," he said, "how about $450,000—in cash?" Hall thought for a moment and then replied, "I'll take it."

"A Lot of Changes and a Few Mistakes"

The announcement of the sale, officially completed on September 28, 1955, was accompanied by Leach's statement that Jack Tar Hotels intended to immediately invest more than $100,000 in renovations of the forty-two-year-old hotel. Sammons and his first wife, Rosine, visited the Grove Park Inn a few weeks later, while plans were being formulated. The inn was closed that winter as workers, under the direction of Leach and the newly appointed general manager, George Stobie, undertook the hotel's first major renovation. Looking back, Leach explained: "We made a lot of changes and a few mistakes, but it was 1955 and we wanted to bring people back to the Grove Park Inn. People didn't care about historic old hotels then. They wanted new, modern motels and we had to recognize that. We decided that the stone columns in the lobby were dust-catchers, so I got ahold of a Miami decorator—or, I should say, a Miami decorator got ahold of me—and talked me into covering the columns."

Elaine D. Sammons worked with her husband, Charles Sammons, to preserve the historical character of the Grove Park Inn, later leading the company after his death.

At the center of each of the six columns in the Great Hall is a square, solid-concrete core that helps support the roof's weight. Before stonemasons applied the granite facing in 1913, the plumbers and electricians had attached, according to Fred Seely's instructions, water, drain, and electrical lines to each of the concrete cores. To replace many of the aging lines in 1955, the stones were removed; but in modernizing the Great Hall, the decision was made not to replace them. Instead, using wood, wire, and plaster, the Merchant Construction Company turned each of the square concrete columns into smooth oval cylinders covered with aqua vinyl wallpaper. The granite stones, some still bearing their original mottoes, were incorporated into other parts of the building, where fragments of faded sayings can still be seen. At the same time, the decorators persuaded Leach that the walls of granite boulders flanking each of the two massive fireplaces should be covered; in front of each wall, carpenters constructed a false wall covered in the same aqua vinyl wallpaper. Although this decision to cover the granite walls and pillars put the visual emphasis on the fireplaces, the Great Hall lost its historic charm and character. "That," acknowledges Leach, "was our greatest mistake."

Any original wicker furniture remaining in the Great Hall was moved to the third-floor Palm Court, placed into storage, or shipped to the Jack Tar Hotel in Galveston. The oak paddle-arm furniture, purchased in 1940, was refinished and recovered; modern furniture filled the voids left by the removal of the wicker rockers. The original tile floor in the Great Hall was thoroughly cleaned, and new rugs were laid down. A canvas awning was installed over the Sunset Terrace, unprotected since 1913. Below the south end of the terrace,

Top left. The Great Hall's granite pillars became giant aqua-colored oval columns in 1955, when interior designers attempted to modernize the Grove Park Inn.

Bottom left. Although repainted in contemporary colors during the remodeling of the Sammons era, the Palm Court has remained much the same since 1913.

Opposite. The addition of the swimming pool in 1956 helped the resort attract the growing number of tourists who vacationed in Asheville each summer.

Sammons had a cloverleaf-shaped swimming pool constructed in 1956. The newly appointed chief engineer, Bill Neilson, who had worked at the inn since 1932, recalled that the pool was kept filled throughout the winter when the inn was closed but logs were floated in the water to keep it from freezing. Farther down the hill, the original tennis court was resurfaced, and below it, on the plateau between the two red-tiled pavilions, a Grove Park Inn landmark—a lighted fountain in the middle of a fragrant flower garden—was sacrificed for a second tennis court.

As part of their modernization program, Sammons and Leach created the Dogwood Terrace, a cocktail lounge and restaurant on the southwest terrace overlooking the swimming pool and golf course. The lounge ran the width of the south end of the building, featuring what earlier had been an outdoor fireplace with a protective hammered-copper hood. At the other end of the building, the inn's main dining room, with two open dining areas on separate levels, was also renovated; the floor in the lower portion, three steps down, was raised to place all diners on the same level. The Plantation Room, as it was called after 1955, still featured the original Roycroft lighting fixtures, but they, like nearly all of the inn's hammered-copper fixtures, had been chemically cleaned and polished, a process that removed the

dark patina characteristic of Arts and Crafts metalware. Wall-to-wall carpeting, heavy drapes with wide valances, and new chairs, tables, china, and silverware effectively transformed the original dining room into one that—had it not been for the original Roycroft lighting fixtures, the two massive oak sideboards, and the four corner servers—might have been found in any modern hotel.

In 1956 the inn's new management team made the decision, later criticized, to dispose of some of the original furnishings. It must be noted, however, that the forty-three-year-old furniture was neither old enough to be considered antique nor new enough to be considered contemporary. The now-famous "G.P.I." dining chairs, with the three initials carved across the crest rail and the Roycroft "R" carved on the back post, were sold to the public for $4 each. The majority of the four hundred chairs were purchased by Asheville citizens and for years afterward could be seen on porches around the city, in one of the local bars, and lining the hallway of a nursing home.

Nearly all of the original White Furniture Company bedroom suites in the 150 remaining guest rooms were retained and refinished. The White rocking chairs with woven cane seats were moved from the rooms to the terraces and porches. Some changes were made to the guest rooms, beginning with the removal of the oak-and-burlap wall treatment on the lower six feet of the walls. This style of decorating, popular during the Arts and Crafts era (1895–1929), when the inn was designed, was considered outdated and unsanitary by the mid-1950s. The oak beds were also altered, first by cutting down the tall footboards and later by removing them altogether. Roycroft ceiling lights with glass globes were left intact, but any fixtures with solid-copper bottoms were modified to accommodate either round glass globes or flat glass panels. The original copper-domed shades of the Roycroft desk lamps, three of which had been placed in each room, were replaced by parchment or cloth shades.

Several of the guest rooms in the north and south wings had always shared connecting bathrooms, designed by Fred Seely for families traveling with children and nannies. More important than a private bath in 1913 were two large trunk closets, necessary for holding the clothing required for an extended stay. Leach proposed to turn the extra closet in each room into a private bath. Wall-to-wall carpeting was installed in a few of the guest rooms, but most of the rooms, which featured a center slab of concrete (intended to be covered by a rug) and an outer band of tile, were decorated with new rugs. As a final touch, each of the guest rooms was outfitted with new linens, from bedspreads and sheets to curtains and towels.

The Inn Meets the Motor Age

The newly renovated Grove Park Inn opened for business in April 1956 under George Stobie's direction, once again as a seasonal resort that was closed for the winter from November until early April. Even before the first guests arrived, including Vice President Richard Nixon

and the Reverend Billy Graham, plans were on the drafting table for a major addition. Both Sammons and Leach realized that the inn's facilities were inadequate for conventions requiring a large number of guest and meeting rooms as well as a spacious ballroom. The era of long-term family guests had vanished, forcing hotels like the Grove Park Inn to compete for conventions to survive. "We recognized from the beginning that we needed to add rooms," Leach observed, "but we also knew that people were flocking to the newest rage—motels. We didn't want—and couldn't have if we tried—to turn the Grove Park Inn into a motel, but we made the decision to build Fairway Lodge next to it so that hopefully we could attract new business."

The two-story motor lodge was designed by Thomas Price, a Texas architect who had assisted Sammons and Leach with the inn's remodeling plans. The site they selected was southwest of the original main building,

adjacent to the new swimming pool and offering guests a panoramic view of the eighteen-hole golf course. Leaving undisturbed many of the pine trees planted in 1913, Price was able to design a semisecluded addition while providing the modern conveniences the public demanded. Covered walkways led to the swimming pool and the Sunset Terrace, providing guests with convenient access to the restaurants and cocktail lounge.

The Fairway Lodge, built at a cost of $200,000, gave the Grove Park Inn an additional fifty guest rooms. In addition, a number of new and remodeled meeting rooms were created at the resort. In the original south wing, where in 1913 there had been four parlors, a writing room, and management offices—all transformed into small meeting rooms before World War II—the Laurel Room and the Green Room were created, both available for meetings, presentations, or formal banquets. An adjacent kitchen served both of

Opposite and right. The main building of the Country Club of Asheville (renamed in 1944), which was adjacent to the Grove Park Inn, was designed by H. T. Lindeberg and constructed in 1926. Fifty years later the clubhouse and grounds became a part of the resort. Club members were permitted to use the facility until 1978, when their new clubhouse in north Asheville was completed.

these rooms as well as the Dogwood Terrace, which is known today as the Carolina Cafe.

On the inn's lower level, the room that had originally housed the indoor swimming pool was remodeled and named the Grotto Room. The room where guests forty years earlier had bowled and played billiards became the Cherokee Room, and the original auditor's office and Fred Seely's first office were transformed into the Mountaineer Room. All were intended to be used for meetings and convention activities. Several years later, all of these lower-level rooms became offices for various departments of the hotel staff.

The Sammons expansion program continued into the 1960s with the construction of the North Wing, built during the winter of 1963 and opened in April 1964. Designed primarily to provide the inn with a spacious ballroom and two more meeting rooms, the North Wing added another forty-six rooms, bringing the total number of guest accommodations to 238. Unlike the Fairway Lodge, the seven-story North Wing was directly attached to the main inn, projecting to the west in the area now occupied by the Vanderbilt Wing. The Plantation Room and the kitchen behind it compelled the architect to design a covered walkway leading from the Sunset Terrace to the new addition. Once inside the 5,456-square-foot ballroom, guests found nothing to indicate that the new facility was even remotely connected with the 1913 Grove Park Inn. The painted woodwork, elaborate crown moldings, formal drapes, blue carpeting, and polished brass lighting fixtures, described in promotional literature as "exquisitely detailed in the tradition of the Carolinas," was inspired by the Federal era of the late eighteenth and early nineteenth centuries rather than the Arts and Crafts era of the original inn.

Arnold Palmer, an inn visitor, was the first golfer to win the Masters Tournament four times. His appealing personality and bold playing style were largely responsible for making golf a popular television sport.

A Hole in One

Through the untiring efforts of its general managers—George Stobie, who remained at the inn from 1955 until 1964, and later Rushton Hays—the Grove Park Inn began the long climb back to respectability. These two general managers built a strong staff that, along with a greatly improved facility, encouraged many conventions, groups, and guests to return to the inn. In 1968, however, Sammons sold six of his hotels, including the Grove Park Inn, to the Osias Resort Hotels Corporation. Although the new owners announced ambitious plans for the Asheville hotel, they lacked adequate financing and strong management. Less than two years later, having done little to improve the hotel, they defaulted on their mortgage, and Sammons once again assumed ownership.

Ed Leach retired as president of the Jack Tar Management Company a Sammons subsidiary, in 1968, and for the next ten years the staff at the Asheville resort watched as a series of general managers came and went in quick succession. Without consistent leadership, the Grove Park Inn, which still operated only from April to November each year, began to stagnate. In Dallas, Sammons's financial empire continued to expand, eventually branching out into cable television, commercial printing, advertising, bottled spring water, health insurance, travel services, and oil-drilling supplies. The Jack Tar Hotels Corporation expanded as well, with an emphasis on full-service beach resorts. Increasing demands on his time and energy made it impossible for Sammons to spend more than a few weeks each year at the Grove Park Inn. The initial spurt in convention business after the opening of the North Wing in 1964 soon sputtered, primarily because of the inn's limited facilities and lack of consistent internal management. By the early 1970s rumors of an impending sale again began to swirl around the hotel, despite achieving the honor of being added to the National Register of Historic Places in 1973.

In 1976 Sammons faced one of his most difficult decisions regarding the Grove Park Inn. It had become increasingly apparent that the inn could not evolve into a world-class resort using a borrowed golf course. More than one convention group had either vowed never to return or had spurned an invitation to meet at the inn because the resort did not have its own golf course. Sammons recognized what Edwin Grove had known as early as 1911: the success or failure of the Grove Park Inn as a resort hotel would, to a large degree, be determined by the availability of a quality golf course for its guests. Since 1913 the members of the adjacent Country Club of Asheville (its new name after 1944)—whose heritage could be traced back to the 1894 Swannanoa Country Club— had tried to work with the inn's owners to make the eighteen-hole course available to hotel guests, but the arrangement was seldom ideal for either the club or the hotel.

Jack Nicklaus was the first player to win all four of golf's major titles at least twice: the British Open, the U.S. Open, the Masters Tournament, and the Professional Golf Association (PGA) tournament.

Although various owners of the Grove Park Inn, including Sammons, attempted to purchase the club's land and buildings over the years, the club refused to relinquish control of the property. In 1976, however, Mitchell Wolfson, a Miami millionaire, initiated a proposal that would unalterably affect the future of the Grove Park Inn. Wolfson, who had built a multimedia empire from a single Miami movie theater, had spent part of nearly every summer in Asheville. He acquired more than one hundred acres of rolling pasture around Beaver Lake, where he raised Angus cattle and thoroughbred race horses. In the early 1940s, to prevent developers from destroying the scenic splendor of the north Asheville area, he bought the bankrupt Beaver Lake golf course. Anticipating that the course might be destroyed after his death, Wolfson formulated a plan to ensure its future.

Negotiations consumed several months, but Wolfson's plan, known around Asheville as "The Big Swap," was essentially quite simple. On November 18, 1976, the Country Club of Asheville agreed to sell to the Jack Tar Hotels Corporation for approximately $2.9 million its eighteen-hole golf course and all of the buildings, land, and facilities associated with it. The club then proceeded to purchase from Lakeview Properties, a Wolfson-owned company, the Beaver Lake golf course for approximately $1,675,000, a figure that even by conservative estimates was well below the actual market value of the land. The club's profit generated from the two transactions was immediately invested in the construction of a new clubhouse and other improvements on the Beaver Lake property. Club members were permitted to continue to use the facilities and golf course adjacent to the Grove Park Inn for the next two years while their new building was being constructed. Then, in 1978, the facility below the inn was renamed the Grove Park Country Club.

For Sammons, the decision to invest nearly $3 million in the purchase of the club property represented an even greater affirmation of his commitment to transform the Grove Park Inn into a world-class resort hotel. As he soon discovered, the addition of the golf course and country club facility provided a foundation for future expansion that would dwarf all he had done since 1955 for the historic inn.

ONE TRUE HERITAGE

⇢ 1978-1991 ⇠

*We talked to several designers until we found someone who appreciated the Inn as much
as we did. Mr. Sammons and I wanted them to make the new wings look as much like
the old as possible by duplicating the Roycroft furniture and by using authentic antiques.*

ELAINE D. SAMMONS
May 3, 1991

Gazing up at the Grove Park Inn from Kimberly Avenue in 1978, a casual observer might never have suspected the problems looming behind its granite walls. News of the purchase of the Country Club of Asheville's golf course two years earlier had reassured local citizens that Charles Sammons had no intention of abandoning the sixty-five-year-old hotel. But serious structural problems in all three of the resort's buildings—the main inn (1913), the Fairway Lodge (1958), and the North Wing (1964)—were either ignored or hastily patched rather than properly repaired. In addition, it soon became apparent that the clubhouse adjacent to the golf course was in far worse condition than anyone had expected. Termites had so weakened the walls that the picturesque clubhouse, some feared, would have to be demolished.

Contending that he had little experience in the hotel industry, Sammons certainly had neither the time nor the insight to recognize his investment's quiet deterioration. Most of his general managers opted for a quiet departure once it became clear that they could not deal with the mounting problems.

Like his predecessor, Edwin Grove, with whom he shared many similarities, Sammons was not immune to personal tragedy. In 1962 his wife, Rosine, had fallen to her death in their new home. For several months afterward, Sammons busied himself with projects outside Dallas. The Jack Tar Hotels Corporation owned resort property in the Bahamas, which continued to present new challenges. Sammons began making regular trips to the resort, spending time in the Jack Tar sales office in

Opposite. After demolition of the outdated North Wing, bulldozers carve out the hillside in the spring of 1987 to prepare for construction of the inn's new Vanderbilt Wing.

Preceding pages. The Sammons Wing, erected on the site of the Fairway Lodge, opened in April 1984. Rather than overshadow the historic building, the new guest wing was purposely designed as an architectural continuation—with the undulating curves of the new structure's red shingled roof extending below the roofline of the original building.

On September 23, 1982, Charles Sammons, Elaine Sammons, and Herman von Treskow, the Grove Park Inn's general manager since 1978, unveiled plans for the 202-room Sammons Wing addition to the resort.

Miami on his way. There he renewed his acquaintance with one of his employees, Elaine Schloff, who had worked for the corporation for several years before and after her first husband's death. Friendship evolved into romance, and in November 1963 they were married.

In 1978, as yet another management change was being contemplated, Peter Street, one of Sammons's advisers, learned of a young man who was looking for the opportunity to manage an American hotel. Herman von Treskow, a native of Posen, Germany, had been trained in the European fashion and was a graduate of the famed Heidelberg hotel management school in Germany. In October 1978, at the age of thirty-four, von Treskow and his wife, Margaret, arrived at the Grove Park Inn. "We flew in here with two babies, four suitcases, and no idea what to expect," he recalled.

Sammons and his new general manager faced a serious challenge. Once the pride of Asheville, the Grove Park Inn had become outdated. Sammons soon became aware of what the inn's engineering staff had known for years: the twenty-year-old Fairway Lodge had not been designed for winter occupancy, and the hastily constructed North Wing was already starting to develop problems. The main inn was in trouble, too. Far less had

actually been accomplished in 1955 to solve serious plumbing and electrical problems than had been thought; what little had been done beyond the cosmetic was already deteriorating. The electrical system was dangerously overloaded, the pipes leaked, and the heating system in the guest rooms ranged from erratic to nearly nonexistent. The inn was in dire need of a complete overhaul, but Sammons was not about to turn his back on it. He was determined to bring all of his resources to bear on restoring and preserving the Grove Park Inn.

Homing In on Heritage

Confident that the inn could be saved, Sammons and von Treskow began making plans for its vigorous revitalization, which would be financed by the owner's many other successful ventures. He and his wife made regular trips to Asheville from their home in Dallas. With her extensive experience in hotel management, Elaine Sammons took a special interest in the Grove Park Inn and the challenges it presented. Both realized that the Grove Park Inn was caught in the ambiguity of being a historic 1913 inn married to a 1958 motor lodge. Too small to attract conventions and too large to survive without them, the hotel would require more than just a fresh coat of paint to survive.

Ever since her first visit to the Grove Park Inn, Elaine Sammons had encouraged her husband to undertake not simply a remodeling but, more important, a historical restoration designed to preserve the property's heritage. Rather than attempting to disguise its age behind plaster and paint, she suggested emphasizing the inn's historical character. Architectural details unique to the era in which it was designed and constructed—granite walls, oak woodwork, Arts and Crafts furniture, and copper lighting fixtures—would be preserved and duplicated throughout the main inn and subsequent additions. "Mr. Sammons and I loved Asheville, we loved the climate, and we knew the Inn could be made even better than it was," she said, "and it was time to do it."

Their first task was the restoration of the main inn. With his wife's encouragement and insight, Sammons had grown more cognizant of the inn's historical significance. Much had been done—and left undone—during the inn's 1955 renovation that now demanded their attention. Starting in 1978, hundreds of feet of water and electrical lines were replaced, the antiquated heating system was improved, and the famous elevators were preserved and rebuilt. The granite walls and concrete floors presented innumerable challenges during the renovation, a process that took several months. Included in the plan was a bar in the Great Hall. In 1979, after North Carolina lawmakers had passed a bill permitting liquor by the drink, a bar was constructed in the southwest corner to serve guests in that room and on the Sunset Terrace. But this outdoor porch presented its own problems. Guests in the rooms overlooking the Sunset Terrace would flip cigarettes out their windows, burning holes in the canvas awning; a sudden shower would send diners scurrying into the Great Hall. By the spring of 1980, however, a permanent roof designed in the same style of the main inn gave the hotel what seemed like a new room.

In undertaking a major expansion program while at the same time restoring the main inn, Sammons did what few other owners would have done. Once the 1913 building had been stabilized, the second step in the revitalization project was expansion—which had to begin with demolition. Charles and Elaine Sammons developed a plan to transform the Grove Park Inn into a major hotel, attracting both large conventions and social guests. To achieve their goal, the inn needed approximately five hundred guest rooms and a wide array of convention facilities, including additional restaurants, ballrooms, and meeting rooms. Standing in their way, however, was the Fairway Lodge. Designed at a time when motor lodges were popular, the two-story structure no longer seemed appropriate next to the historic inn.

A proposal was made to demolish the motel and construct in its place a 202-room addition with more than 11,000 square feet of meeting space—all designed to complement rather than clash with the original inn's architectural style. Charles Sammons listened intently as the plan was presented and then asked, "How much is it going to cost?" "Twenty million dollars," was the reply. Sammons, who had originally paid but a small fraction of that amount to buy the hotel, asked only for his wife's assurance that she would oversee the project. Then he said, "Do it."

One Falls, Another Rises

On November 15, 1982, at the close of the hotel's regular season, the piers beneath the twenty-four-year-old Fairway Lodge were dynamited, and the structure tumbled down the slope of Sunset Mountain. In a matter of hours, bulldozers had begun to clear away the remains of the ill-fated addition and prepare the hillside for the foundation of the new Sammons Wing. Seventy years earlier on that same slope, Fred Seely, Oscar Mills, and the first construction crew had built the main inn using teams of mules and a single steam shovel. In sharp contrast, the Daniel Construction Company commandeered cranes and even a helicopter to assemble the nine-story addition.

Rather than overshadow the historic building, the Sammons Wing was designed as an architectural continuation, the undulating curves of its red shingled roof extending below the roofline of the original structure. The top floor, which contains the Heritage Ballroom, a lounge, a restaurant, and several meeting rooms, appears to be an extension of the Great Hall. The eight lower guest floors are built into the hillside overlooking the eighteen-hole golf course. Included in the plans for the Sammons Wing was an indoor swimming pool, for Elaine and Charles Sammons had decided to reopen the Grove Park Inn as a year-round resort for the first time since the mid-1950s.

While the contractor assembled the steel skeleton of the Sammons Wing, another crew renovated the main inn, including the Great Hall. Workers tore down the oval facades wrapped around the six concrete columns, replacing plumbing and electrical lines as they progressed. The decision to recover the six columns, the north and south walls, and the front desk with oak rather than granite (which had been removed or covered during the winter of 1955) was carefully thought through; in the end, it was agreed that the Great Hall could be improved by the color and texture of oak paneling over a return to the monotony of an all-granite, all-gray interior. The small floor tiles, which had begun to break loose and disappear, were replaced with slabs of gray slate, duplicating the color of the original floor with a material natural to the mountain region. The same slate continued uninterrupted throughout the lobby level of the Sammons Wing. The transition from the old to the new was further accomplished by using granite stones on the new interior walls. Only a close inspection reveals where the original stonework stopped in 1913 and the new began in 1984.

On her arrival in 1963, Elaine Sammons had put a stop to the practice of discarding and selling original furnishings handcrafted by the Roycroft Shops and the White Furniture Company. She instructed Design Continuum, interior designers from Atlanta, to purchase authentic Arts and Crafts antiques, including Morris chairs, box settles, sideboards, and china cabinets by Gustav Stickley, Charles Limbert, and L. and J. G. Stickley, as well as quality reproductions to fill the Great Hall

Left. Construction of the Sammons Wing began in the fall of 1982. Inspecting the new wing in May 1983 are (left to right) Herman von Treskow, Charles and Elaine Sammons, and Joe Kanewske, vice president of Sammons Enterprises.

Opposite. History repeats itself: in the spring of 1984, as stonemasons complete the final wall outside the Sammons Wing, General Manager Herman von Treskow (left) uses a wagon pulled by a team of horses to haul the final load of boulders. To his right is Jimmie Stepp of Stepp's Stone Works.

and Sammons Wing lobby. To maintain harmony between the original inn and the new wing, scores of Arts and Crafts antiques were added, creating a smooth flow between the two sections. The antiques also allowed the Grove Park Inn staff to point with pride to the largest collection of authentic Arts and Crafts furniture and lighting fixtures in the entire country.

But the crowning glory of the new Sammons Wing was the 8,778-square-foot Heritage Ballroom. Elegant yet functional, the ballroom, like the entire wing, was designed and decorated to complement, not compete with, the historic inn. Oak woodwork, carefully selected draperies and carpets, and custom-designed copper chandeliers handcrafted in the Arts and Crafts style provided the perfect backdrop for the delicate balance of authentic antiques and accurate reproductions. The ballroom could seat one thousand diners, and its carefully planned and positioned kitchen could also service the inn's most elegant new restaurant, Horizons.

When, on April 20, 1984, the newly renovated and expanded Grove Park Inn opened its doors for year-round occupancy, it had much to offer: 410 rooms, three restaurants, two lounges, two ballrooms, expanded convention facilities, and something no amount of money could construct—a proud history.

Phases Three and Four

Restoration of the main inn and completion of the Sammons Wing signaled the beginning of the third phase of the Sammons plan: renovation of the country club. Increased business from regional and national corporate conventions, as well as vacationers in the Blue Ridge Mountains, would create additional demands on the hotel's golf course and clubhouse. The rambling, Norman-style clubhouse, built in 1926, had badly deteriorated; what began as a remodeling project quickly evolved into an extensive restoration, as workers discovered termite damage throughout the entire structure. Once again, Elaine Sammons provided the leadership and Charles Sammons the financial support—more than $1 million—

to renovate the clubhouse, restaurant, outdoor swimming pool, and golf course. When the facility reopened on June 11, 1985, the Grove Park Inn could point with pride to one of the finest country clubs in the state.

Yet even before the country club renovation was complete, a new structure was being built on the hotel grounds. Little more than one hundred yards east of the main inn, across from the original site of Sunset Hall (a staff dormitory razed in the 1980s), a 32,514-square-foot Sports Center was under construction. Recognizing that the original building's integrity could not be protected while providing space for a modern sports facility, the owners had it built at a distance. This completely separate facility opened on December 22, 1985, giving guests that winter the opportunity to enjoy two racquetball courts, three tennis courts, a squash court, a weight training room, an aerobics room, whirlpools, and saunas.

Although the addition of the golf course, Grove Park Country Club, Sammons Wing, and Sports Center had transformed the hotel into a full-service resort and conference center, owners Charles and Elaine Sammons

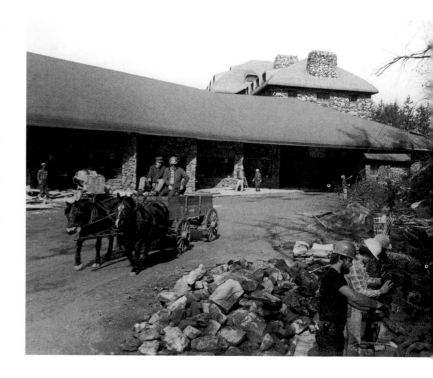

remained dedicated to their goal of a five-hundred-room resort. On December 15, 1986, detonation charges carefully placed around the North Wing's foundation neatly dropped the seven-story structure at the foot of the inn without damage to the seventy-three-year-old granite walls. Once again, bulldozers and construction crews descended on the site, paving the way for the final phase of the Grove Park Inn's expansion.

Drawing their inspiration from both the historic building and the Sammons addition, the architects and interior designers of the 413,250-square-foot Vanderbilt Wing gracefully blended the old with the new. Once again, the soft roof lines reflected those of the main inn and remained below the original red tiled roof. The Vanderbilt Wing connector was designed to display antiques, documents, and photographs from the Grove Park Inn's past. The walkway to the Blue Ridge Dining Room was paved with gray slate and decorated with Arts and Crafts antiques, accurate reproductions, and hammered-copper lighting fixtures.

Located more than one hundred feet above ground, the new Blue Ridge Dining Room provided guests with panoramic views of the Asheville skyline and distant mountains. The addition of this four-hundred-seat restaurant changed the role of the original Grove Park Inn dining room. After carefully removing the original Roycroft chandeliers, wall sconces, and massive oak buffets for installation in the Blue Ridge Dining Room, workers remodeled the Plantation Room into staff offices. Although over the course of seventy-five years it had served five presidents and scores of dignitaries, the Plantation Room was too small and its kitchen too outdated to make the transition from serving three hundred guests to an anticipated one thousand diners.

The eleven-story Vanderbilt Wing provided the Grove Park Inn with 166 new guest rooms furnished with reproduction Arts and Crafts oak furniture, but its primary purpose was to offer convention facilities that would rival or surpass any in the Southeast. To complement the Heritage Ballroom in the Sammons Wing, the Grand Ballroom, on the eighth floor in the Vanderbilt addition, offered 17,676 square feet of convention hall space capable of seating more than two thousand persons. With the official opening of the Vanderbilt Wing and the completion of the expansion program, the Grove Park Inn's statistics were impressive: 140 acres of grounds, 510 guest rooms, five restaurants and lounges, two ballrooms, forty meeting rooms, a country club and eighteen-hole golf course, two swimming pools, indoor and outdoor sports facilities, more than six hundred employees, and an annual payroll in excess of $10 million. And located in the center of it all is the jewel in the Grove Park Inn crown: the historic main inn.

Charles Sammons died at the age of ninety on November 12, 1988, less than three months after the opening of the Vanderbilt Wing and the successful completion of the ambitious $65 million expansion and renovation program he had financed. Although his business empire was estimated to be worth in excess of $2 billion, he had remained throughout his life a shy, quiet man, content to give those who worked in his organization the opportunity to manage his businesses as if they were their own. He maintained his home in Dallas, where he gave generously to numerous charitable organizations, particularly in medicine and the arts, but he and his wife continued to visit North Carolina on a regular basis, for they, like many others, maintained "a love affair with Asheville"—and the Grove Park Inn.

Sammons's death marked the end of an era of tremendous expansion for the seventy-five-year-old Grove Park Inn. Three years later, on June 12, 1991, Herman von Treskow left his post of general manager after nearly thirteen years. Without Edwin Grove in 1912, the inn would never have been built. Without Charles Sammons in 1955, it might never have been saved. These two men and the thousands of people who have worked at the Grove Park Inn since the first shovelful of dirt was turned on July 9, 1912, made it possible for countless numbers of guests to breathe clean air, walk amid tall pines, warm themselves before a blazing hearth, and take home treasured memories of a journey to the Grove Park Inn.

The stage was set for the Grove Park Inn's march into a new century.

THESE ENCIRCLING MOUNTAINS

➤➤ 1991 TO THE PRESENT ◄◄

If it weren't for the vision of Mrs. Sammons, we'd still be a 270-room inn that was only open seven months of the year.

J. CRAIG MADISON
President and Chief Executive Officer
The Grove Park Inn Resort and Spa

With the death of Charles Sammons in November 1988, many observers and hotel staff predicted that the Grove Park Inn would soon pass into the hands of a major hotel conglomerate. For months afterward, rumors of an impending sale flew throughout the hotel and filtered down to Asheville. In recent years the Sammons Corporation had divested itself of many of the twenty-two hotels and resorts that Charles Sammons had purchased over the years; at the time of his death, the magnate owned only six hotels in addition to the Grove Park Inn. Many predicted that Elaine Sammons, his widow, who became the Sammons Corporation's newly elected board chairman, would soon follow the advice of financial advisers who were urging her to shed the seventy-five-year-old hotel and the maintenance challenges it presented.

What the prognosticators failed to accurately assess, however, was Elaine Sammons's determination not only to keep the Grove Park Inn but also to guide it to an even a higher level of service and excellence while maintaining the commitment she and her husband had made years earlier: to preserve the heritage of the historic hotel. Fulfilling this commitment would require unwavering dedication in the face of complex structural problems as well as the influx of millions of dollars of improvements made even more difficult and more costly by her personal determination not to sacrifice the unique charm, personality, and history that distinguish the Grove Park Inn.

Opposite. With its new wings, spa, and golf course, the Grove Park Inn has taken its place among the elite list of resort hotels that have set themselves above all others.

Preceding pages. In 2002 the Grove Park Inn's golf course was restored to the plan designed in 1926 by the famed Scottish golf course architect Donald J. Ross. Also visible in this photograph are two recent historical acquisitions: the Curtis Bynum House and the sprawling Battle Mansion (bottom right and bottom left, respectively).

With the completion of the Sammons Wing in 1984 and the Vanderbilt Wing in 1988, the Grove Park Inn had grown to 510 rooms, fifty thousand square feet of meeting space, two expansive ballrooms, four restaurants, and two lounges. However, compared to these new spaces, with their gleaming woodwork and new Arts and Crafts carpeting, draperies, antiques, and reproductions, the historic main inn was again beginning to show its age. In 1991 Elaine Sammons and her new general manager, James France, began making plans to revive the hotel's first building.

A New Facelift for the Old Inn

Fred Seely's Palm Court on the inn's third floor—originally furnished with wicker furniture and four massive Arts and Crafts oak planters with towering palm trees—had become a depository for mismatched furniture. Using historic photographs as a guide, the staff turned its attention to restoring the court. They began with the meticulous removal of thirteen layers of paint covering a section of Arts and Crafts stencils applied to the parapet walls. Over the course of several weeks, Mark Ellis-Bennett, an Asheville craftsman and artist, painstakingly researched, uncovered, and duplicated the original stenciling using many of the same techniques and materials from 1913. Crews next repainted the walls, restored the original oak planters, installed Arts and Crafts–style carpets, and replaced the furniture castoffs with reproduction wicker rockers and settees appropriate for an Arts and Crafts room. Examples of original Arts and Crafts furniture made in 1913 by the White Furniture Company for the guest rooms were moved to the Palm Court and adjacent hallways, where they could be appreciated by

The Carolina Cafe, which began as an open terrace in 1913, was enclosed for casual dining and named the Dogwood Cafe during the 1950s. The Roycroft sconces on the stone walls were moved from the inn's original dining room when it was remodeled in 1988.

Opposite. With the completion of its permanent roof in 1978, the resort's Sunset Terrace has become one of the most popular dining spots in the region.

Above. The Grove Park Inn's menus continue to reflect Fred Seely's original concern for healthy, high-quality foods.

Right top and bottom. Among the resort's options for elegant dining are the Sammons Wing terrace and the country club.

Below. At the end of the Sammons Wing can be found the inn's most formal dining room, Horizons Restaurant.

guests. In 1996, in recognition of its restoration of the Palm Court, the Grove Park Inn Resort (so named after 1993) was presented with a Griffin Award by the Preservation Society of Asheville and Buncombe County.

To bring in sunlight and create a natural ventilation system for the Palm Court, Fred Seely and Edwin Grove had installed in the peak of the hotel's roof a massive skylight the entire length of the Palm Court. The original skylight could be opened in summer months to provide an escape for warm air as well as a pleasing breeze of fresh, mountain air through each of the rooms, but by 1999 it was creating problems. With the installation of air conditioning in the guest rooms, the movable glass panels had been sealed and several others covered in an attempt to reduce the amount of heat that accumulated in the court as sunlight streamed through the glass. The original sky-

light was also susceptible to leaks, so in 1999, while crews were working on the roof, a crane operator deftly lowered a new, custom-designed skylight into place.

The final stage in the main inn's interior renovation was completed in January 2001, when the last of the surviving 150 original rooms were stripped down to their bare walls and completely refurbished. As an indication of her commitment to preserving the inn's original elements, Sammons decided that rather than removing and replacing the original wooden windows, craftsmen would meticulously repair broken parts, rebuild rotted sections, and reglaze individual panes—thus preserving the historical integrity of the guest rooms and the structure's exterior. The original Arts and Crafts oak dressers, nightstands, desks, and chairs were also restored while workers installed new carpeting, draperies, and wall coverings.

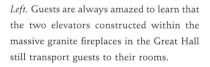

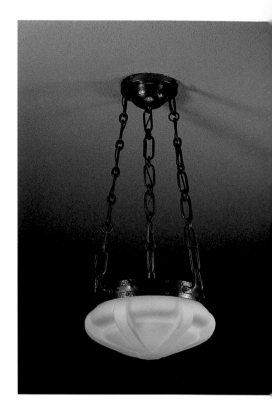

Left. Guests are always amazed to learn that the two elevators constructed within the massive granite fireplaces in the Great Hall still transport guests to their rooms.

Top center. In 1913 the Roycrofters produced large copper lanterns for the terraces surrounding the inn. These later provided the inspiration for many of the new lighting fixtures in the Vanderbilt Wing.

Top right. Victor Toothaker, a Roycroft artist and metalsmith, designed several styles of lighting fixtures for the hotel, including glass-and-copper chandeliers such as this for the guest rooms and hallways.

Right. One of the original "G.P.I." chairs from the Roycrofters is displayed in the memorabilia exhibit in the Vanderbilt Wing connector. The exhibit, part of the Grove Park Inn archives, preserves the history of the inn and its many famous guests.

The famous eight-foot-tall Roycroft clock has stood in the Grove Park Inn since 1913. In all likelihood, the quote on the front of the clock, like those on the hall's boulders, was selected by Fred Seely.

Finally, a new Arts and Crafts armoire was designed and crafted for each room, deftly concealing a television set, stereo equipment, a microwave oven, a refrigerator, and a coffee maker, while reinforcing the appearance of an Arts and Crafts room from 1913.

Downstairs, workers were following Sammons's instructions for refurbishing the Great Hall. Numerous projects were completed over the course of several years, beginning with the addition of an oak bar inspired by the Arts and Crafts style, the remodeling of the front desk area, and the repair of the original fireplaces. Ellis-Bennett returned to duplicate a ceiling stencil design, restore the faded quotations Seely had selected to be painted on rocks on the walls and fireplaces, and repatinate the copper hardware on the eight-foot-tall 1913 Roycroft oak clock. The inn's Arts and Crafts antiques were restored as well; Stickley and Roycroft Morris chairs and rockers were recovered in fabrics reflecting the Arts and Crafts style. In addition, reproduction Arts and Crafts table lamps were selected to supplement the light from the historic Roycroft chandeliers hanging from the ceiling since 1913.

After much debate the decision was made to leave, at least for the time being, the oak boards encasing the Great Hall's four massive concrete pillars. Originally wrapped with stone, the concrete pillars still served as a means of leading and supporting water pipes, plumbing, wiring, and telephone lines to the original guest rooms off the Palm Court. Because the oak boards had been milled and finished in the Arts and Crafts style and provided easier access than stone to the plumbing and electrical lines behind them, they were kept as they had been since 1964.

While work continued throughout the historic building, Sammons initiated plans for a $1.4 million refurbishment of the ten-year-old Sammons Wing, including new wallpaper and draperies, Arts and Crafts stenciling on elevator doors, new lighting fixtures in the Arts and Crafts style, and new box springs and mattresses in each of the 202 rooms. Not unlike Seely eighty years earlier, Sammons personally selected the

Arts and Crafts carpeting and draperies for the guest rooms and the hallways.

Renovation plans extended to the historic structure's exterior as well. The famous red tile roof, while complicated, served the inn well until the mid-1990s, when serious problems had begun to appear. Chronic leaks resulted in extensive damage to the plaster ceiling and walls in the sixth-floor guest rooms. The flashing between the tiles and the chimneys had deteriorated, and many of the tiles had either cracked or come loose. It became obvious that the tiles would have to be replaced, but Sammons had to decide whether to opt for less-expensive asphalt shingles or for 440,000 replacement clay tiles. She never hesitated.

Workers began removing the original tiles in 1999 and discovered, as they had expected, that the wooden battens holding the tiles on the roof were nearly all rotted. The concrete itself, which had been poured without

consistent quality control, had also deteriorated badly. After patching the concrete, the crew covered the roof with a waterproof membrane and a new latticework of water-resistant lumber attached to the concrete with special screws. At that point eight trained craftsmen began the meticulous task of covering the undulating roof, including each of the sixth-floor dormers, with clay tile, just as had been done in 1913. The project consumed eighteen months of work and cost more than $3 million but preserved the inn's original appearance.

By 1999 the Sports Complex, which opened in 1985 with indoor tennis courts and a pool, was similarly in need of a major overhaul, as well as additional facilities. After an expenditure of more than $3 million by Sammons, the complex reopened that year with a new swimming pool; three indoor and three outdoor tennis courts; separate weight, cardiovascular, and aerobic rooms; a racquetball court; and a children's playground and activities room.

Opposite. In 1999 workers begin removing the original red clay tile roof covering the main inn. The eighteen-month project repaired the poured-concrete roof and included replacement of its clay tiles.

Above. A small group of specially trained workers use a spider-web system of ropes and harnesses to maintain their footing on the roof as they begin replacing the historic building's original tiles.

Right. J. Craig Madison, president and chief executive officer of the Grove Park Inn Resort and Spa, installs the final clay tile on the main inn roof in 2000.

Prelude to the Third Millennium

The year 1999 also marked a pivotal turning point for management of the Grove Park Inn Resort. That September Elaine Sammons named as the resort's new general manager J. Craig Madison, an Asheville native who in 1978 had cofounded the Alpha Group, a local advertising agency. Since 1979 the Alpha Group had created and directed numerous successful advertising campaigns for the hotel. Madison had also served as the inn's director of marketing since 1984. During its tenure, the Alpha Group won more than one hundred awards for creative excellence for advertising projects designed for the Grove Park Inn. Although Madison, like his distant predecessor Fred Seely, had never managed a hotel before, his extensive knowledge of the inn, his familiarity with Sammons's goals for the hotel, and his ability to motivate a staff of more than one thousand persons made the transition nearly seamless.

It fell to Madison and his staff, most notably Troy Hunnicutt, director of development, to carry Sammons's vision for the resort into the twenty-first century. The goal remained to preserve its historic fabric as the country's most heralded Arts and Crafts hotel while transforming it into one of the most popular destinations for families, conferences, and businesses. Even while the roof scaffolding still surrounded the hotel and its soothing roofline was rudely interrupted by the presence of a towering crane, Madison and Sammons were preparing the Grove Park Inn Resort to embark on its most ambitious project ever: a 40,000-square-foot, world-class spa.

The idea for the spa came from Sammons herself. "I had been traveling around and found that most of the finer resorts have spas," she recalled. "I thought that the Grove Park Inn needed a spa, for it is the trend of the future." The challenge she and her designers faced, however, was to append a readily accessible spa onto a historic hotel without damaging the integrity of the main inn or blocking the view of the

Opposite: While work continued on the roof of the main building, in 1999 another crew began preparing the site below the Sunset Terrace for the Grove Park Inn's new spa envisioned by Elaine Sammons.

Above and right: The spa's architect, Robert LeBlond, suggested building the new facility underground to avoid blocking the historic inn or guests' mountain views. After two years of construction, the luxurious subterranean spa opened in 2001.

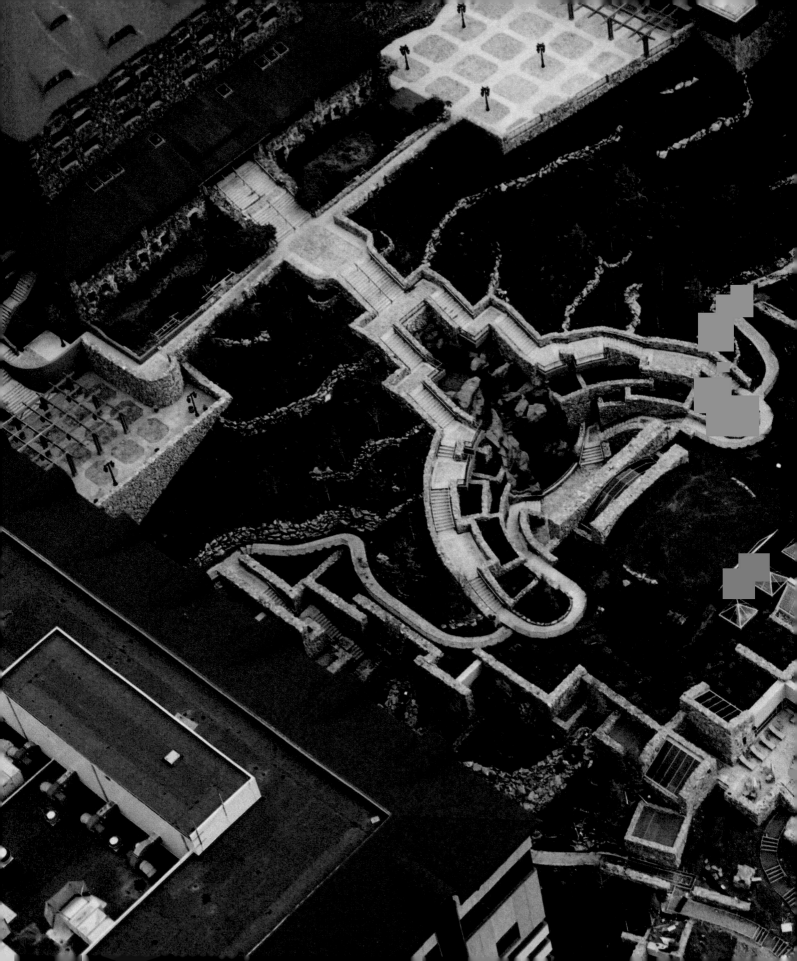

Blue Ridge Mountains. Robert LeBlond, an architect with LeBlond Partnership Architects and Planners, designers of the Banff Springs Hotel Solace Spa in Canada, came up with a novel solution: build the spa underground.

Taking his inspiration from the original structure itself, LeBlond designed a subterranean spa made almost totally of stone, drawing on indigenous themes of fire, sky, water, and stone as his concept developed. The spa was located directly beneath the steps leading down from the Sunset Terrace to a pair of existing tennis courts and two small pavilions. Both the tennis courts and the pavilions were removed to make way for the spa, but additional courts were added to the Sports Complex, and the pavilions were rebuilt. LeBlond's design called for a three-story building and a complex plumbing, heating, and electrical system built entirely underground and topped by a series of stone steps, waterfalls, skylights, plantings, and boulders at nearly the same slope as the original approach to the Sunset Terrace.

Construction of the underground spa took nearly two years, during which time the cost rose from an initial estimate of $12 million to a final tally of more than $42 million. Sammons remained philosophical throughout the process. "Everything costs more than you expect it to," she commented, adding that she felt determined that the Grove Park Inn Resort should build a spa as fine as or better than any other resort spa.

After the laying of the last of eight million pounds of stone, the spa opened on February 28, 2001. An "oasis of luxury set within the landscaped courtyard below the

Walkways from the main building, the Vanderbilt Wing, and the Sammons Wing lead guests past a series of waterfalls and into the spa's main entrance. Rock walls and abundant plantings on the roof of much of the spa make a nearly seamless transition from the golf course to the original inn.

hotel," the subterranean spa is connected to the Sammons and Vanderbilt Wings by underground corridors and to the main inn by a series of circular, descending stone steps that pass through a landscaped courtyard complete with a majestic, cascading waterfall, pools, and natural gardens. Once inside the flagstone-paved spa reception area, guests discover a variety of pleasing amenities, including a spa cafe, a specialty spa boutique, and an exercise room. A vaulted ceiling frames a large window offering a tempting glimpse into the main spa pool below. Both the men's and the women's changing areas feature fireplace lounges and additional views of the pools and the Blue Ridge Mountains. In the architect's own words, the spa at the Grove Park Inn Resort blends "hand in glove with the hotel's unique architecture, historical significance and natural setting and reflects our design philosophy that architecture is

based on more than wood and stone—the spa will be real living architecture."

As Craig Madison's first year as general manager of the Grove Park Inn Resort drew to a close, plans were completed for a Grand Millennium Celebration designed to herald the new century with a three-night bash. The hotel was closed to the general public so that the staff could devote themselves entirely to the millennium activities, which included the jazz favorites Cleo Lane and John Dankworth, the Drifters, the comedians Robert Klein and David Brenner, the blues icon Percy Sledge, and a $50,000 fireworks show at the stroke of midnight on New Year's Eve. To commemorate the event, the resort commissioned David McHugh, a faculty member at the North Carolina School of the Arts and a noted Hollywood composer, to compose "The Grove Park Inn Prelude and Overture to the Third Mil-

Opposite: A waterfall below the historic Grove Park Inn signals the watery delights that await in the new underground spa.

Above and right: A sinuous, mazelike pool greets visitors to the spa enclave, which enjoys spectacular views of the Blue Ridge Mountains. Beyond, a glass-roofed pavilion beckons for additional sybaritic pleasures.

Above and left: Conjuring up an underground grotto, the spa has been described as a magical place that has long existed yet has just been discovered. Guests can relax in the pool while gazing up at thousands of fiber-optic stars twinkling in the rocks overhead. Also available are pools with contrasting hot and cold temperatures.

Opposite: One popular spa treatment is a couple's massage in the open-air Pagoda. Grove Park guests can also choose to have aura imaging and color and light therapy.

lennium." It had its world premiere at the resort on New Year's Eve and was recorded by the North Carolina School of the Arts Symphony Orchestra and Cantata Singers.

During the 1990s, a decade of restoration and expansion at the Grove Park Inn Resort, the staff continued to serve its guests with the high quality of service for which the hotel had always been noted. In addition to attracting families, business travelers, meetings, and conventions during the most popular seasons, the resort also initiated a series of Adventure Weekends during the months of January and February. Madison and his staff recognized that to draw guests during the winter months, they would need to organize a series of annual activities, ranging from educational conferences to pure entertainment.

The first of the Adventure Weekends was introduced in 1988 with the inaugural national Arts and Crafts Conference and Antiques Show. Designed for collectors of the popular Arts and Crafts style of furniture, pottery, metalware, and art, the event was a natural match for the Grove Park Inn. Its success encouraged the addition of other Adventure Weekends using the hotel's indoor facilities, including the annual Heritage Classic Dance Sport Championship starting in 1988, the Comedy Classic Weekend in 1989, the Big Band Swing Dance Weekend in 1993, the All That Jazz Weekend in 1994, and the Best of Our State Weekend in 1999. As a result, what had once been considered a slow time of year for the resort has become one of the most popular.

Left. The noted Scottish golf course designer Donald J. Ross is memorialized in an outdoor statue at the Grove Park Country Club. The eighteen-hole championship golf course owes its origins to his 1913 redesign of an existing course. His work inspired the golf course architect Kris Spence to completely revise the entire course in 2001.

Below. With its high-pitched roof, the 1926 clubhouse, originally home to the Asheville Country Club, drew its inspiration from Norman villas in France. The building and golf course were transferred to the Grove Park Inn in 1976 and restored ten years later.

Opposite. This aerial view shows work in progress during the golf course renovation in 2001—a transformation that the director of the Donald Ross Society has called "as good as I have seen, anywhere." Now returned to Ross's intentions, the course presents a more historical appearance that recalls its days of welcoming golf greats from the 1920s to the 1950s.

Although Edwin Grove had once owned more than twelve hundred acres of land surrounding the Grove Park Inn, by the year 2000 all but 149 acres had been developed into residential neighborhoods, taken over by the golf course, or transferred to the adjacent Biltmore Industries. Frustrated by their inability to provide adequate parking during many of the Adventure Weekends and other special events, Sammons and her management team felt the need to explore other options beyond the inn's present boundaries.

The resort's nearest neighbor, the S. Westray Battle House, stands just a short distance from the front entrance to the grounds. Built in 1927, a few months after Grove's death, the sprawling three-story stucco structure was once one of Asheville's finest homes. Beginning in 1954, however, the sixteen-room house was converted into a television station and offices and was later further compromised by an incongruous addition and numerous insensitive remodelings. When

the station owners in 1998 announced their intention to move to larger quarters, they offered the building and property to Sammons. Despite having no immediate plans for the property, she purchased the sprawling structure.

Adjacent to the Battle House, at 200 Macon Avenue, is the Curtis Bynum House, designed in 1924 by the architect Ronald Greene. This stately home was built of random-coursed granite blocks highlighted by a slate roof, a circular stair tower, and entrances faced with Indiana limestone. Designed with a commanding view of the French Broad River valley and downtown Asheville, the house became available in 1998 and was purchased the following year by the resort. Conversion into a bed-and-breakfast inn was considered, but projected costs of more than $1 million dollars to create just five guest rooms grounded the project. Other options included moving it to another site, but each idea was rejected in turn. Both the Bynum and Battle Houses await completion of a master plan for the entire Grove Park Inn property.

Soon the golf course called out again for attention. Sammons made the decision to close the course completely on June 1, 2001, and, under the direction of the golf course architect Kris Spence, a specialist in renovating original Donald Ross designs, had the course restored to Ross's intentions. During the next eighteen months and at a cost of more than $2 million, Spence and his staff reworked the entire course, restoring the crowned putting greens with deceptive contours (a Ross trademark), making the bunker locations more challenging, removing unwanted trees, and installing heat-resistent bent grass on the tees and fairways as well as on the putting greens. The result was a course with a more traditional 1920s flavor, one reminiscent of when it was a regular stop on the Professional Golf Association tour, from 1933 until 1951, and of exhibition matches by such famous golfers as Ted Ray and Harry Varden in the 1940s and Jack Nicklaus, Sam Snead, and Arnold Palmer in subsequent years.

Today the Grove Park Inn Resort and Spa has taken its place among the elite list of resort hotels that have set themselves above all others. When Seely declared in 1913 that the Grove Park Inn was "the finest resort hotel in the world," he could not have known that nearly a century later it would still wear that coveted crown. Few other resort hotels in the world can offer the same blend of history and modern conveniences, convention facilities tastefully incorporated into an intimate atmosphere, a 40,000-square-foot spa without parallel, and a complete sports facility steeped in history.

On the night of July 12, 1913, William Jennings Bryan, one of the Grove Park Inn's first and most faithful guests, captured the essence of what Edwin Wiley Grove and Fred Seely had built and what Charles and Elaine Sammons have saved, restored, and expanded. All of them saw their task not as building for one generation or one century but "for the ages."

The main inn and the Sunset Terrace can be seen from the Sammons Wing terrace. Seasonal open-air dining and colorful vistas at sundown have long made this spot a favorite with guests.

⟿ RECENT EMPLOYEES OF THE GROVE PARK INN ⟾

30+ Years of Service

Name	Years Employed
Harwood, Linda	1974–
Henderson, Susan	1975–
Hipps, Maxine	1970–2004
Payne, Norman	1962–1998
Payne, Peggy	1959–1999
Rowland, Edna	1963–2005
Shands, Alfonzo	1968–2006

25–29 Years of Service

Name	Years Employed
Baker, Freda	1979–
Buckner, Kenneth	1976–
Green, Dorothy	1960–1985
Leyva, Sheila	1981–
Madison, Craig	1978–
McHone, Noe	1981–
Smith, Luci	1981–
Williams, Barbara	1974–2001

20–24 Years of Service

Name	Years Employed
Allen, Carl	1985–2005
Anderson, Ruth	1984–
Ball, Kevin	1986–
Ball, Robert	1977–1999
Bates, Dorothy	1984–
Campbell, Angela	1984–2006
Carpenter, Becky	1986–
Chamberlain, Robert	1984–
Dawi, Fred	1985–
Evans, Margie	1984–
Freck, Thomas	1984–
Gibson, Barbara	1979–2000
Griffis, Peggy	1985–
Hamner, Reni	1984–
Harris, Kathy	1986–
Hazel, Shelia	1985–
Hoyt, Selvin	1985–
Hunnicutt, Troy	1986–
Marshall-Lance, Mary	1975–1998
Metcalf, Patsy	1985–2006
Moore, Elijah	1985–
Morin, Ron	1984–
O'Mary, Robert	1984–
Patigas, Pedro	1986–
Porter, Dolores	1986–
Pounders, Michael	1984–
Reece, Donovan	1986–
Scales, Theodore	1984–
Seamon, Mary	1985–2003
Stewart, Jack	1984–
Sullivan, Hedy	1984–
Thomas, Terry	1985–
Wilkerson, Bobby	1984–

15–19 Years of Service

Name	Years Employed
Acerenza, Louis	1990–
Anders, Shelby	1980–1999
Aquino, Fermina	1991–
Arredondo, Teofilo	1990–
Arvizu, Manuel	1990–
Bailey, Johnny	1990–
Baird, Teresa	1991–
Baker, Priscilla	1990–
Baker, Stan	1990–
Ball, Arley	1990–2002
Ball, Grace	1990–1998
Blackwell, Albena	1990–
Boyd, Jay	1991–
Brady, Donald	1990–2000
Brady, Sandra	1987–2002
Briggs, Emory	1991–
Brown, Donald	1984–2003
Brown, Herman	1990–
Brumley, Bobby	1990–2005
Calvin, James	1982–1997
Carter, Patty	1990–2005
Cartwright, Brenda	1990–
Cline Harwood, Carol	1990–2005
Cogburn, Jean	1990–2006
Corn, Tracey	1991–
Craig, Joseph	1986–2001
Craig, Martin	1990–
Creasman, Ernest	1976–1996
Dawkins, Wallace	1990–
Donaldson, Ivan	1985–2000
Fisher, Pam	1990–
Fox, Hazel	1984–2000
Gaddy, Ethel	1965–1984
Gamble, John	1990–2000
Gentry, Dianna	1991–
Gentry, Richard	1990–
Gibbons, Michael	1990–
Gibbs, Karen	1984–1999
Gossett, Robert	1990–
Hanson, Stephanie	1990–
Hensley, Bernice	1991–2006
Hensley, Mary	1967–1984
Hernandez, Manuel	1990–
Hoglen, Mary	1991–2006
Hollifield, Lane	1990–2004
Jochetz, Traci	1990–2004
Johnson, Amy	1990–
Kelley, William	1990–
Lance, Theron	1990–2003
Medford, Ricky	1990–2001
Morrow-Simpson, Debbie	1990–
Moss, Jeff	1989–2004
Myers, Billy	1990–
Neatherway, Ian	1990–2000
Neff, Terry	1990–2001
Ownbey, Lou	1990–2005
Papay, William	1990–
Parsons, Teresa	1990–2004
Piccirillo, Jeff	1990–
Pressley, Randall	1990–
Price, Terry	1990–
Quinones, Enrique	1990–
Rice, Mary	1990–2003
Roberts, Erlinda	1986–2001
Roberts, Linda	1990–
Roth, Tim	1990–
Ruff, Michael	1990–
Sams, Mary	1990–
Sanders, Al	1977–1992
Schlubach, Maggie	1982–2001
Shelton, Susie	1987–2006
Smith, James	1989–
Snelson, Dorothy	1990–
Tate, Navajo	1987–
Thomas, Antonio	1985–2001
Wampler, Angelica	1990–
Whitener, Ethan	1990–2004
Whitener, Sandra	1990–
Whitten, Helen	1986–2004
Wright, Betty	1985–2000
Wykle, James	1988–

10–14 Years of Service

Name	Years Employed
Adams, Harlon	1988–2002
Anderson, Antoinette	1993–
Anderson, Jack	1988–2002
Arredondo, Olivo	1990–2000
Arroyo, Gilberto	1995–
Arthur, Matthew	1994–
Atkins, Stewart	1993–
Avery, Wendy	1996–
Ball, Christy	1993–
Ball, David	1980–1991
Ball, Tony	1992–2003
Banks, Christy	1995–
Barnes, Derrick	1990–2000
Bastardo, Mercedes	1991–2002
Beckett, Emily	1996–2006
Bishop, Judy	1987–2001
Blocker, Harold	1989–2001
Boone, Shawn	1996–
Bowers, Thomas	1992–
Bridges, Patricia	1991–2001
Brown, Beverly	1994–
Brumfield, Suzanne	1991–2001
Burns, Lynn	1986–1999
Calfee, Jill	1996–
Cantrell, Jr., Alec	1992–2005
Carpenter, Glenna	1985–1996
Carson, Linda	1987–2000
Carter, Doug	1985–1997
Castlewitz, Sue	1981–1992
Chapin, Edwin	1985–1998
Clodfelter, Daisha	1995–
Conley, Minnie	1989–2001
Conyers, Robert	1986–2001
Creasman, Roger	1994–
Crisp, Wendy	1992–

Davis, Judy	1994–	Mitoraj, Stanley	1987–1998	Yakima, Michael	1983–1993
Davis, Linda	1990–2002	Moore, Larry	1990–2003	York, Patsy Lee	1984–1996
Diaz, Francisco	1995–	Morgan, Martha	1992–	Young, David	1989–2000
Donaldson, Sylvia	1985–1999	Morris, Don	1982–1994	Zuniga, Manuel	1994–
Dougall, Kathleen	1994–2004	Novo, Tony	1982–1996		
Duncan, Gay	1987–1998	Nunez, Rosendo	1995–		
Drury, Robert	1985–2000	Owenby, Shirley	1982–1992		

5–9 Years of Service

Name	Years Employed
Edwards, Teresa	1988–1998	Palmer, Douglas	1995–	Adair, Allen	1994–2000
Erskine, David	1979–1990	Phookhamnerd, Rungrit	1994–	Adams, Jonathan	1998–
Escobedo, Juan	1993–	Price, Lueva	1993–	Alavez, Beth	2000–
Escobedo, Refugio	1994–	Prieto, Nicolas	1996–	Alexander, Bert	1998–2005
Finley, Hazel	1992–	Raiford Jr., Dalton	1991–2005	Allison, William	1991–1999
Frantz, Michael	1992–	Ramos, Luis	1996–	Anderson, Erik	1999–2005
Freeman, Eugene	1992–2004	Ramsey, Floyd	1981–1991	Anderson, Hazel	1999–
Gaddy, Randall	1988–1999	Ramsuer, Isolda	1994–	Anderson, Sandra	1989–1996
Gamboa, Yelka	1992–	Rattler, Judy	1991–2001	Angell, Sue	2000–
Garcia, Jose	1995–	Raymer, Hank	1991–2001	Anuel, Zurilma	1999–
Gardner, Gary	1985–1997	Reese, Vicki	1986–1999	Argueta, Doris	1999–
Gothard, Diann	1991–	Reichard, Betty	1993–2003	Arnold, Rebecca	1997–1995
Gowing, Ronald	1993–	Reid, Vickie	1988–2000	Ascencio, Esteban	1993–1998
Green, Janet	1994–	Rhodes, Lisa	1984–1994	Atkins, Nelson	1994–2004
Groleau, Jacques	1994–	Ridley, Elizabeth	1991–2002	Banks, Lucille	1992–2001
Guerra, Pedro	1996–	Rivera, Felipe	1993–	Banks, William	1993–2001
Hamilton, Lynnette	1989–2002	Roberts, Brent	1983–1994	Banning, Autumn	1992–1997
Hardy, Henry	1978–1990	Romano, Betty	1986–2000	Barrows, Jason	2001–
Hargett, Virginia	1985–1996	Ross, Sharon	1995–	Barry, Christine	1985–1992
Haynes, Robert	1984–1998	Rowe, Jane	1978–1991	Baylor, Gail	1986–1993
Herrera, Justa	1996–	Rowland, David	1996–	Bennett-Kuster, Kathleen	1992–1997
Herrera, Max	1987–2002	Sampson, Greg	1992–	Benton, Greg	1999–
Hudson, Vickie	1987–2001	Sams, Gerald	1988–2000	Bickerton, Robert	1988–1994
Husch, Susan	1989–2002	Santaella, Flor	1996–	Black, Bobby Joe	1985–1991
Inscoe, Libby	1988–1998	Schronce, Scott	1996–	Blalock, Hazel	1999–2006
Israel, Louise	1992–2005	Schwartz, Kevin	1991–	Bogan, Rosamund	1987–1993
Ivey, Deborah	1995–	Selman, Jade	1986–1997	Bolick, Virgil	2000–2006
Jackson, Jean	1976–1987	Shelton, Geraldine	1989–2003	Bonar, Erin	1999–2006
Janis, Claudia	1990–2004	Shipman, Ruth	1992–	Boseman, Virginia	1988–1995
Jones, Carolyn	1987–2001	Simpson, Brian	1995–	Bowden, Natasha	2001–
Jones, Jane	1989–2003	Snyder, Geraldine	1986–1999	Bradley, Terri	1989–1994
Kapustka, Wojciech	1988–2000	Solesby, Kermit	1988–2002	Brigman, Deborah	1985–1990
Krickhan, William	1976–1991	Sprowles, Susan	1994–	Brown, Ben	1986–1993
Lankewich, Maureen	1989–2004	Stafford, Bobby	1986–2001	Brown, Betty J.	1991–1998
Larkin Jr., James	1988–1998	Stamey, Jane	1989–2003	Brown, Betty R.	1993–2000
Lawrence, Dennis	1993–	Stevens, Peggy	1995–	Brown, Geethanjal	1986–1994
Layton, Ethel	1988–2000	Stish, Mary-Fran	1995–2006	Brown, William	1988–1997
Ledford, Howell	1987–1998	Styles, Bobbie	1986–1997	Brown, Wrought	1985–1991
Ledford, Kenneth	1990–2005	Swinnerton, Pam	1994–	Buckner, Dawn	1992–2000
Llamas, Casimiro	1992–	Tipton, Suzanne	1982–1993	Buckner, Hilda	1985–1991
Llamas, Jorge	1994–2004	Torres, Epifania	1993–	Buckner, Lynne	1986–1992
Llamas, Socorro	1995–	Tschudy, Rose Mary	1988–1999	Buerer, Kathleen	2001–
Lollis, Leonard	1985–1999	Van Ryn, Joyce	1989–1999	Burgin, Rob	2000–2005
Lutomski, Kevin	1994–	Vogel, Johannes	1982–1992	Candelario, Maria	1994–2001
Maldonado, Miguel	1995–	Von Treskow, Herman	1978–1991	Carpenter, Nevin	2000–
Mason, Mark	1990–2001	Watley, Arthur	1988–2001	Carpenter, Randy	1986–1993
Mayeux, Ray	1994–	Watts, Henry	1989–2000	Carpenter, Rebecca	1998–2004
McCurry, Joey	1996–	Wegenka, Julie	1993–	Carrera, Maria	1999–
McElrath, Doris	1984–1997	Welch, Darrell	1983–1996	Carter, Larry	1980–1989
McIntosh, Pamela	1994–	Wharey, Lois	1983–1993	Cash, Andrew	1992–1997
McLeod, Donald	1987–1998	Williams, Kim	1992–	Chamberlain, Julius	1997–2003
McMinn, Karen	1993–	Willis, Chadwick	1995–	Chandler, Carolyn	1989–1995
Meadows, John	1996–	Wilson, Cynthia	1984–1994	Charlier, Nate	2000–
Metcalf, Garold	1985–1995	Wilson, Donnie	1987–2000	Cindric, Zrinka	1994–2002
Meyer, Suellen	1977–1990	Wilson, Johnnie	1996–	Clark, Ann	1994–1999
Miller, Cornelius	1986–2000	Wise, Cynthia	1995–	Clark, Benjamin	1999–2004
Miller, John	1990–2003	Wright, Herman	1989–2001	Clark, Carol	1994–1999
Miller, Valerie	1990–2004	Wyatt, Alice	1987–1997	Clark, Gene	1998–
Minker, Vivian	1973–1985	Wynegar-Sauer, Gene	1977–1992		

Clark, Frederick	1992–1999	Freeman, Susan	1993–2000	Johnson, Mary Margaret	1996–2002
Clark, Kingston	1999–	Freeman, Thomas	1990–1997	Johnson, Timothy	1992–2000
Clark, Lee	1992–1999	French, Elizabeth	1998–2003	Jones, Frederick	1996–
Clark, Willie	1998–	Gagner, Hugh	1996–2005	Jones, James	1986–1993
Claveau, Martin	1999–	Gant, Christopher	1996–2002	Jones, Owen	1994–2000
Clement, Lureatha	1984–1989	Garber, Donna	2001–	Jones, Sonja	1984–1992
Coggins, Kristie	1998–2003	Garrison, Brian	1998–	Jordan, Connell	1991–2001
Cole, Jeffery	1994–1999	Garrison, David	1999–	Keagy, Larry	1995–2004
Colley, Gwen	1998–	Garrison, Michael	1990–1997	Keaton, Lewana	1984–1991
Collins, Barbara	2000–	Gibson, Christine	2000–	Kelley, Barbara	1989–1994
Contento, Janet	1998–	Gillen, David	1992–2000	Kelly, Patrick	1989–1996
Conti, Darlene	1988–1995	Gilmore, Virgil	1999–	Kelton, Kelly	2001–
Cooley, Chris	1988–1995	Glenn, Paul	1999–	King, Alan	1987–1996
Cooper, Caroline	1988–1993	Gonzalez, Gilberto	1997–2003	King, J., Ryan	1992–1997
Cooper, Drew	2000–	Good, Matt	2001–	King, Robert	1987–1995
Cordell, Corky	1997–2006	Gordon, Vickie	1998–	Kinsella, Andriette	2001–
Corriveau, Carol	2001–	Gosnell, Christina	1993–2001	Kirk, Barbara	1999–2005
Costner, Karen	1992–1999	Grader, Rob	2000–	Klaas, Douglas	1998–2006
Crawford, John	1981–1989	Grant, Tracy	2001–	Klaas, Kim	2000–2006
Crockett, Tarry	1999–2006	Gray, Janice	1998–2004	Knapton, Courtney	1999–2005
Crowder, Ben	1997–2004	Gray, Walter	1989–1996	Knight, Larry	2000–
Cullen, Charles	1993–1998	Green, Mary	1992–2000	Knighton, David	1996–2004
Curtis, Amanda	2001–	Griffiths, Judith	2000–	Knutson, Jerry	1995–2000
Curtis, Cindy	1991–1999	Grubby, Dorothy	1999–2004	Koch, Brittany	2000–
Dacko, Timothy	1994–2000	Gryder, Angela	1990–1998	Kulik, Nataliya	1997–
Dalton, Terry	1989–1995	Gryder, William	1994–2000	Ladd, Deborah	1998–2006
Davis, Ronda	2000–	Guerra, Marina	2000–2006	Ladd, John	1996–2003
Davis, Tony	1995–2000	Guerra, Roberto	1993–1998	Lally, Carter	1993–2001
Dean, Brenda	1993–1998	Guerra, Rosario	1993–2001	Lamont, Barbara	1984–1990
Debrew, Revella	1988–1996	Guerra, Severiano	1991–1998	Lane, Jennifer	1997–2004
Debruhl, Caroleen	1997–	Guerra, Silviano	1993–2000	Langford, Roy	2000–
DeLeon, Pedro	1993–2000	Guevara, Carlos	1999–	Laughlin, Pola	1998–
Denton, John	2000–	Gunter-Gosnell, Sandra	1985–1990	Leeseberg, Fred	1999–
De Rivera, Pabla	1998–	Gusman, Jose	1993–1999	Lindberg, Jenny	1992–1999
Dominguez, Rosa	2000–2006	Hagan, Marjorie	1987–1994	Lindenaux, Renee	2001–
Dorn, Phyllis	1998–2005	Hall, James	1999–	Lindstrom, Carol	1998–
Dougall, John	1994–1999	Haltof Jr., Fred	1989–1998	Littlejohn, Brenda	1998–
Downey, Joseph	1997–	Hamer, Charlie	1999–	Llamas Flores, Luzmaria	1998–
Drury, Darlene	1996–2004	Hamlett, Clyde	1990–1997	Lloyd, Laverne	1989–1998
Duncan, Denise	1989–1997	Hammond, Bradley	1996–2002	Lockridge, Samuel	1996–2002
Dunn, Richard	1991–1999	Hanlon, Richard	1994–2002	Logan, Diane	1996–
Dy, Olena	1998–	Harper, Matthew	1996–2004	Logan, Roxanna	1991–1998
Early, George	1994–2000	Harris, Nancy	2001–	Lomeli, L. Abel	1992–2001
Eddings, Derrick	1994–2000	Hartmus, Raleigh	1991–1998	Longoria, Betsy	2001–
Edwards, Jim	2001–2006	Hechler, Jerry	1986–1991	Loughmiller, Karen	1994–2000
Edwards, Victoria	1985–1993	Heinrich, Kathleen	1999–	Lunsford, Hazel	1989–1998
Ehrlichman, Dwight	1990–1997	Hensley, Kari	2001–	Lybarger, Laurie	1995–2000
Eisweirth, Joseph	1994–2001	Hensley, Rickey	1988–1997	Lynn, Celeste	1999–
Eley, Mike	2001–	Hernandez Pino, Jorge	1993–2003	Lyons, Mark	2000–
Ellenburg, Kenneth	1989–1998	Herrera, Justa	1996–	Mack, Darryl	1991–1996
Elliott, Carlos	1988–1994	Hofmann, Peter	1994–2003	Mahaffey, David	1987–1993
Ensley, Katy	1988–1994	Holland, Hollis	1995–2002	Maher, Claudia	1988–1995
Escobar, Juan	1992–1998	Honeycutt Jurczyga, Brandy	2001–	Manley, Elizabeth	1999–
Everson, Janet	1985–1990	Hookstra, Annmarie	1995–2000	Manley, Jose	1998–
Farthing, Ian	1998–	Hornes, Asenath	1998–2006	Mapp, Howard	1993–1998
Fickes, Marc	1997–2003	House, Karen	2001–2006	Marsh, Jerlene	1992–1998
Finley, Belinda	1992–1999	Hosking, Deborah	1999–	Martinez, Antonio	1992–1999
Fisher, Joshua	1998–	Huffman, Jaime	2001–	Martinez, Miguel	1993–1998
Fitzpatrick, Kimberly	1992–1998	Hughes, James	1992–1997	Martin-Simes, Julie	1995–2001
Fitzpatrick, Shawn	1991–1998	Hughes, Joseph	1998–	Massie, James	1993–2000
Forsyth, Kenda	2000–	Hyatt, Clyde	1987–1994	Mauldin, Carroll	1992–2000
Fowler, Kenneth	1997–	Ivey, Christopher	1998–2006	Mays, William	1992–1999
France, James	1991–1999	Jackson, Amy	1999–	McBee, William	1993–2000
Franklin, Patricia	1988–1998	Jackson, Henry	1983–1990	McCormick, Kim	2000–
Freeman, James	1987–1994	James, Julie	1991–2001	McCrea, Carolyn	2000–
Freeman, Phyllis	1991–1997	Jenkins, Linda	2001–	McCurry, Tiffeny	1996–

McDonald, Eugene	1978–1983	Pressley, David	1997–2006	Stamey, Charles	2000–2005
McDougal, Darlene	1999–	Pressley, Vicki	1993–2000	Steuber, Gary	2000–
McIntyre, Nancy	1994–2000	Pritchitt, Pat	2001–	Stokes, Anthony	1990–1997
McKenzie, Lauren	1993–2001	Proctor, Karen	1991–1996	Stransky, Brooke	2001–
McKenzie Jr., Dedrick	1985–1990	Proctor, Richard	1993–2001	Sullins, Gregory	1990–1995
McKeown, Patrick	1998–	Putzel, Mary	1994–1999	Sweeney, Isabel	1976–1984
McKinney, Dawn	1993–2001	Queen, Deanna	1999–	Sweezy, Carolyn	1984–1990
Meadows, Frank	1999–2005	Raisley, Kate	1999–2004	Swing, Derrick	1997–
Membreno, Angela	1997–2004	Ramirez, Florencio	1990–1997	Taylor, Amanda	1999–
Menjivar, Maria	1996–2002	Rangel, Victorino	1990–1998	Terry, Shelley	1997–2005
Messer, Kenneth	1985–1991	Reed, Francis	1992–1998	Tetrault, Daniel	2001–
Metcalf, Ethel	2001–	Reeves, Linda	1985–1993	Thomas, Clinton	1989–1995
Metcalf, Juanita	1997–2005	Resper, James	2001–	Thomas, Mary	1990–2000
Michele, Eric	1998–	Rhom, Brigitte	1990–1996	Toms, Terri	1998–
Milam, Rodell	1985–1993	Rice, Larry	1997–	Tomsky, David	1994–2002
Miller, Betty	1990–1999	Rinker, Richard	1997–2004	Torio, Carlito	1989–1997
Miller, Timothy	1997–	Rivas, Santos	1999–2005	Trantham, Dennis	1992–1997
Mills Jr., David	1989–1994	Rivera, Paula	1998–	Trantham, Golda	1997–
Minter Jr., George	1995–2001	Roberts, Diane	1983–1990	Treiber, Hubert	1989–1996
Moberg, Paul	2001–	Robertson, Delores	1994–2000	Trejo, Mary	1998–
Mobley, Steven	1993–1999	Robertson, William	1994–2000	Unanue, Michael	2001–
Moffett, Joni	1992–2002	Robinson, Chief	1999–2004	Vecchione, Lena	1996–2001
Montgomery, James	1991–2000	Robinson, Michael	1999–	Velez, Carlos	2000–2005
Moore, Jack	1986–1991	Robinson, Timothy	1995–2001	Vernon, Magina	1989–1998
Morey, Melissa	2001–	Roccaforte, John	1998–	Wagar, Kim	2001–
Morgan, Aaron	1997–	Runkle, Tasha	2001–	Waldroup, Roy	1986–1995
Morgan, Ben	1991–2000	Sanchez, Margarita	1991–1999	Walker, Connie	1988–1995
Moyer, Lloyd	1988–1997	Sanford, Kimberly	1992–1998	Walker, Davis	2001–
Mullen, Brendan	1999–	Santiago, Elisa	1998–	Walker, Pleas	1996–
Mulligan, Jason	1995–2001	Savage, Stephen	1990–1997	Walker, Robert	1999–2006
Munoz, Yolanda	2001–	Schaerer, Roland	2001–	Walker, William	1995–2004
Murphy, Tracie	1989–1998	Schmidt, Roger	1993–2002	Wallen III, Robert	1992–1999
Naret, Mike	2000–	Schwartz, Christina	1988–1996	Walters, Amy	1999–
Navarrete, Elvira	1999–	Shade, Trellis	1989–1994	Walton, John	1986–1995
Nolan, Beverly	1990–1998	Shahriari, Elizabeth	1998–2003	Ware, Roger	1987–1992
North, Pamela	1999–2005	Shambaugh, Keith	1994–1999	Warner, Jeanne	1983–1993
Nunez, Manuel	1997–	Shearhod, Greg	1992–1997	Watkins, Ernest	1990–1999
Nunez, Nancy	1997–	Shelley, Terry	1997–2005	Watkins, Sandy	1998–2004
Oates, Rickie	1995–2001	Shelton, Kyle	1990–1998	Watson, Matthew	1989–1994
Osteen, Clara	1987–1997	Shoemaker, Jon	2001–	Weber, Raymond	1997–
Pace, Faith	1998–2004	Siegel, Harry	1997–	Welch, Patricia	1995–2003
Paegelow, Karen	1991–1997	Silver, Shelly	1990–1996	Wells, Oksana	1997–
Pagony, Lajos	1985–1991	Silvers, Marie	2001–2006	Whisman, Glenda	1990–1996
Papierski, Joyce	1986–1992	Simes, Erik	1997–2006	Whitmire, Karla	1994–2001
Parham, Dorothy	1987–1994	Slagle, Robert	1996–2002	Wilcox, Donald	1996–2002
Parlett, Dave	2001–	Sloan, Valerie	1993–2000	Wiley, Charlena	1988–1993
Parsons, Paul	1998–	Sluder, Grace	1986–1995	Wilkie, Kimberley	1990–1997
Pascal, Jennifer	1991–2000	Smith, Belinda	1998–2004	Williams, Doreen	1991–1997
Payne, Dora	1984–1991	Smith, Elizabeth	1989–1997	Williams, Hollis	1990–1996
Payton, Audrey	1991–1997	Smith, Gail	1985–1992	Williams, Jason	1996–2001
Peek, Heath	2000–	Smith, Glenda	1996–2003	Wilson, Ed	1999–
Perez, Isidro	2000–	Smith, Gregory	1991–2000	Winer, Jay	2000–
Perry, Jamie	2001–2006	Smith, Jane	1983–1993	Winspear, W. Earl	1993–1999
Peterson, Susan	1996–	Smith, Jason	1992–1998	Wintenburg, William	1983–1990
Phillips, Ryan	1999–	Smith, Jesse	1999–	Wolf, Jason	1995–2003
Phillips, Trinity	2001–	Smith, Kasey	2001–	Wolf, Laura	1993–2001
Picard, Christine	1994–2001	Smith, Lilly	1996–	Wolfe, Sheryl	1998–
Pingree, Jay	1996–2001	Smith, Susan	1998–	Womble, Steve	2000–
Plank, Rebecca	2001–2006	Smith, Vonnie	1989–1997	Wooten, Luke	1997–2003
Plemmons, Roger	1988–1998	Smith, Willie	2001–	Wright, Susan	2001–
Ponder, Ricky	1984–1991	Sorto, Maria	1996–	Wyant, Shanda	1994–2003
Ponder-King, Kathie	1984–1992	Sotomayor, Nancy	2001–	Young, Andrea	1998–
Porter, Kato	1997–	Sovinskiy, Mariya	1998–	Young, Margaret	1998–
Porter, Robin	1990–1998	Spencer, Jeffrey	1996–2005	Zimprich, Kim	1995–2003
Powell, Julie	1999–	Sprouse, Kimberly	1995–2002	Zinger, Gerald	1991–1999
Pratt, Valerie	2001–	St. Peters, Jeffrey	1996–	Zink, Brett	1998–2006

⇒ TWO SPECIAL RESIDENTS ⇐

Since 1994 the resort's own "Major Bear" has welcomed children and adults to the Grove Park Inn and made surprise appearances at special events and Adventure Weekends. His legacy goes back to visits in the 1930s by Franklin and Eleanor Roosevelt. Around the turn of the century Eleanor, so the story goes, was given a Teddy bear by her uncle Teddy Roosevelt (the living model for all Teddy bears). This bear, as the story continues, lived in the White House, traveled the world, and played happily with the Roosevelt children until an unfortunate occurrence: according to the legend, he was accidentally left behind after a visit to the Grove Park Inn.

Nicknamed Major Bear, the cuddly creature reappeared toward the end of the twentieth century as a life-size mascot dressed by the puppeteer Hobi Ford. Although the original bear suit endured for seven years, it was not agile, had a limited line of sight, and was extremely warm; in fact, it could be worn only twenty minutes at a time.

In 2001 Sugars Mascots of Toronto designed a more functional and friendly greeter. Today the legend of Major Bear lives on as he continues to delight guests with each appearance.

Some employees and guests also claim to have seen another apparition wandering the Grove Park's halls. Its description has remained eerily consistent: a young woman, seemingly gentle and shy, dressed in a pale, pink gown. A theory arose that the mysterious Pink Lady had fallen to her death in the Palm Court, but no supporting documentation exists. In 1995–96 a group of sleuths into things paranormal tried to catch a glimpse of the elusive spirit and capture on film proof of her existence. The crew emerged—without any sightings or photographic evidence—convinced that the Grove Park Inn is indeed haunted (see *Haunted Asheville,* by Joshua Warren. Shadowbox Publications, Asheville, 1996).

So, is the Grove Park Inn haunted? You'll just have to experience it for yourself.

RESORT EVENTS AND PUBLIC RELATIONS STAFF
The Grove Park Inn Resort and Spa